THE
ANSWER

Making Sense of Life,
One Question at a Time

JENNIFER KRAUSE

A Perigee Book

A PERIGEE BOOK
Published by the Penguin Group
Penguin Group (USA) Inc.
375 Hudson Street, New York, New York 10014, USA
Penguin Group (Canada), 90 Eglinton Avenue East, Suite 700, Toronto, Ontario M4P 2Y3, Canada
(a division of Pearson Penguin Canada Inc.)
Penguin Books Ltd., 80 Strand, London WC2R 0RL, England
Penguin Group Ireland, 25 St. Stephen's Green, Dublin 2, Ireland (a division of Penguin Books Ltd.)
Penguin Group (Australia), 250 Camberwell Road, Camberwell, Victoria 3124, Australia
(a division of Pearson Australia Group Pty. Ltd.)
Penguin Books India Pvt. Ltd., 11 Community Centre, Panchsheel Park, New Delhi—110 017, India
Penguin Group (NZ), 67 Apollo Drive, Rosedale, North Shore 0632, New Zealand
(a division of Pearson New Zealand Ltd.)
Penguin Books (South Africa) (Pty.) Ltd., 24 Sturdee Avenue, Rosebank, Johannesburg 2196,
South Africa

Penguin Books Ltd., Registered Offices: 80 Strand, London WC2R 0RL, England

While the author has made every effort to provide accurate telephone numbers and Internet addresses at the time of publication, neither the publisher nor the author assumes any responsibility for errors, or for changes that occur after publication. Further, the publisher does not have any control over and does not assume any responsibility for author or third-party websites or their content.

First edition: October 2007

Library of Congress Cataloging-in-Publication Data

Krause, Jennifer.
    The answer : making sense of life, one question at a time / Jennifer Krause.
        p. cm.
"A Perigee book."
Includes bibliographical references.
ISBN-13: 978-0-399-53370-9
1. Life.   I. Title.
BD431.K735 2007
128—dc22   2007025202

PRINTED IN THE UNITED STATES OF AMERICA

10   9   8   7   6   5   4   3   2   1

Most Perigee books are available at special quantity discounts for bulk purchases for sales promotions, premiums, fund-raising, or educational use. Special books, or book excerpts, can also be created to fit specific needs. For details, write: Special Markets, Penguin Group (USA) Inc., 375 Hudson Street, New York, New York 10014.

To my grandma,
Irene Sarver,
for whom there is never a question.

CONTENTS

Introduction

Welcome to the jungle, we take it day by day. . . .

—Guns N' Roses, "Welcome to the Jungle"

They say it's a jungle out there. And if ever we've lived in a time of all-powerful "they"s it is now.

"They" are the ones ready with the solutions for everything that keeps us awake at night: How can I lose weight? Get healthy? Find the love of my life? Maintain the love of my life? Snag the right job? Get out of debt? Yet even God, Google, and a gaggle of gurus don't make the questions go away.

We're taking more pills to fall asleep than ever (and asking our doctors for them by name). Store shelves are stuffed with diet and exercise books, but 65 percent of us remain overweight. Countless how-to-quit guides exist to prevent the certain deaths of one of every two smokers, and forty-eight million adults continue to light up each year. The world is awash with answers, so why aren't we—or it—getting better?

As I began writing these words, the title of a book I had read as a child, and hadn't thought of for at least twenty-five years, suddenly came to mind: *A Swiftly Tilting Planet*. As I reread Madeleine L'Engle's tale of a brother-and-sister team uniting to save the world from destruction, my thirty-four-year-old internal "highlighter" lingered over some dialogue I'm certain I moved past rather quickly when I was eight (probably because I had a book report due!). Two characters, exhausted from their efforts, find a large rock where they can rest at the edge of a rough sea. After lying there for a moment, one hesitates and panics a bit, not trusting the place they've found. The other encourages him to stay, saying, "It can be a bit scary, being part of the earth and stars and fireflies and clouds and rocks. Lie down again. You won't fall off, I promise."

The fact is that an ever-changing world and our perpetually evolving lives guarantee that we all share the same piece of real estate, even if we call different parts of the country or the globe home. Our human address is on the edge—of chaos and clarity, of struggle and success, of wandering and wisdom. Rarely gliding through life in our scrubbed-up Sunday best, more often we are dusty from the challenges of day-to-day living. Every time we think we have it all worked out, a new—or an old—question comes along to shake things up and make us feel like we're falling off the edge. Even as we gather experiences that may help us shape our lives more effectively and enable us to face familiar challenges with greater ease, what we know in one moment does not ensure we'll know how to face what's next.

Life is always asking us questions. Our lives are the answers.

We think, though, that it works the other way—that life, or someone else's life, holds the answers, and that we are walking, talking, living, breathing, open-bellied question marks waiting to be filled. Yet it didn't start out that way. At least not in Eden.

According to the Book of Genesis, the whole human project begins with a question. God says, "Shall we make humanity in our image?" But exactly whom is God asking? Birds, insects, trees? And why should God have to ask anyone's permission? The ancients suggest that God is consulting with a heavenly court of angels, emphasizing the importance of asking questions even before the first people arrive on the scene.

And the questions keep coming. After Adam and Eve disobey God's order to stay away from the Tree of Knowledge of Good and Evil, God returns to the Garden of Eden and asks Adam, "Where are you?" God then inquires of Eve, "What have you done?" Surely an all-powerful God would know the answers to these questions, right? No, early scholars say, God wants to engage Adam and Eve in a conversation, wants to encourage their struggle to find answers of their own. God is demonstrating the power of the question—our fuel for life.

If God and the Garden aren't your thing, let's fast forward to the example of famed management consultant Peter Drucker. Drucker left Vienna as the Nazis came into power, and eventually made his way to the United States to become one of the most sought-after voices in business until the last days of his nearly ninety-six years of life. A 2005 *BusinessWeek* article about Drucker published just after he died explained that his style was to tell everyone, including Fortune 500 company CEOs, "My job is to ask questions. It's your job to provide answers." Apparently Drucker expected no less of himself. He once also revealed, "I learn only through listening. To myself." Drucker understood both the power of questions and the invaluable power of answers that come from one's own insides.

Letting questions fuel our lives shouldn't be confused with not acting, or with not making decisions. Obviously it would be ludicrous in a life-or-death situation, for instance, to examine a question from all angles. Take the

Royal Bank of Scotland commercial in which a guy is choking on his food in a restaurant while his dining partners leisurely discuss the relative merits of doing the Heimlich maneuver. These are not the questions I have in mind. Instead, we're going to look at the questions that don't have one-word, final, all-purpose answers—the kinds of questions where the answers not only change in each generation but also at different moments over the course of one individual lifetime:

1. What's to Fear?

2. Am I Good?

3. When Will I Grow Up?

4. Who's Got My Back?

5. Who Has My Heart?

6. What's It All About?

7. Am I Missing Something?

As German philosopher Arthur Schopenhauer wrote in an essay, "On Thinking for Yourself": "A truth that has merely been learnt adheres to us only as an artificial limb, a false tooth, a wax nose does, or at most like transplanted skin; but truth won by thinking for ourself is like a natural limb; it alone really belongs to us." That is why questions—these questions—are the beating heart of human life, and why we must use them to find our own inner wisdom to live the truths that truly belong to us.

Oftentimes spiritual leaders forget that they're human and that they don't "have" the answers. Fortunately the wise people we meet in our work knock us off our pedestals—real or imagined. For instance, a student of mine served up a whopper of a question in a class I was teaching soon after finishing rabbinical school. "What is a rabbi for?" she asked. Now, when I say "a student," you should know that this woman was in her seventies, and, at the time, I was twenty-eight. But I was "The Rabbi," and therefore I was there for the answers—or so I thought. It was my first job out of seminary, and I was teaching for a prestigious national Jewish organization—a position that, as my grandma said, was "a real feather in my cap."

The other ladies in the room jumped in before I even had a chance to respond. "The rabbi is for religion," one argued. "No, no, no," said another, pausing to take a lipstick-kissed sip from her coffee cup. "The rabbi," she said emphatically, "is for life." The rabbi is for life? How was I going to be "for life"? How was I going to make myself a teacher for everyone, someone who could speak from the midst of experience, not just watch from the sidelines, quoting verses and preaching proverbs?

At the time, the notion that my purpose was not to be "the answer woman," as I had imagined my position required, left me feeling more than slightly unsettled. But I couldn't be more grateful for that one question, and for all of the questions ever since, that made *not* having all the answers my best guide. They have inspired me to be more—as a teacher, as a person—than I ever could have been without them. And they have taught me that whenever we learn to use our questions, we find a power that can take us through any challenge we face in life.

Our questions get us to "the more" in everything. They change and make our lives. And we are the most human when we are challenged by these questions; we are the most interconnected when we realize we share the same struggles. Whether through talks with people in the workshops I teach, conversations I have with seatmates on airplanes, or snippets of strangers' cell phone calls I overhear while walking along the sidewalks of New York City, my experience has been that all people—regardless of what they do or don't believe—are buzzing with the same unknowns. We wonder if we're happy, if we're in the "right" relationship, if we're using our time well, what really matters. The questions are the same.

I didn't always know I wanted to be a rabbi, or really start considering the possibility until I was in college. In graduate school, I was taught to teach people. But spending the better part of the last decade speaking all across North America, working as "a rabbi without borders," I've learned how to let people and their lives teach me. And the best teaching I've received—whether in Nashville, Philadelphia, or Cleveland, at Christian prayer breakfasts or Jewish bagel brunches—is that questions are the gateway to new ideas, next steps, and personal breakthroughs. People leave a room more energized when they've chewed on a challenging question, even expanded it, without necessarily reaching one conclusion. They feel more connected to what's happening in their own lives, and closer to the strangers in their midst.

So, yes, I'm a rabbi, but this is not a Jewish book, or a book about religion. Some of the wisdom I reference comes from religious traditions, such as Buddhism, Hinduism, Islam, Christianity, and Judaism. And those ideas may refer to a deity or deities as they appear in their original context. But if there's a term that does not resonate with your belief system, substitute something else that does. It's like the scene from Kenneth Lonergan's film *You Can Count on Me*, in which a priest (played by Lonergan himself) asks his parishioner's brother, Terry (played by Mark Ruffalo) if it's possible for him to believe that his life is "important" and "connected to something" without calling it any one thing that runs contrary to his heart or his intellect. Terry responds, "I don't know, Ron. A lot of what you're saying has real appeal to me . . . but I don't want to believe in something or not believe in it because I might feel bad. I want to believe in it or not believe in it because I think it's true or not."

We have instant access to more information than at any other time in human history, are exposed to myriad ways of thinking and being, and can freely adopt or reject all kinds of traditions and practices. And just as Terry confides to the priest, guilt, fear, and blind obligation are not good enough reasons for us to believe in anything. We need to be free to explore and arrive at our deepest held beliefs without being threatened, duped, or terrified into getting there. The greater puzzle of living can never be complete with one tradition, one approach, or by relying on one "expert" to fill in the blanks. So although I cherish the religious traditions I've inherited, I do not believe that any one religion has cornered the market on the Truth. That is why these pages also include references to music, art, advertising, theater, film, food, television, politics, and poetry—the stuff of all our lives.

This is a book for people who have more questions in their lives than answers. This is a book for people who want to make their lives matter—not just for themselves and the people who love them, but in the larger scheme of things. This is a book for people who want to act in—and maybe even change—the world, but who understand that having core beliefs and having all the answers are two very different things. The world may try and tell us that success means being certain, never revealing ambivalence or ambiguity. Yet even the questions we do our very best to avoid facing have a way of finding us, putting us in places we never would have expected. The toughest questions take us highest, move us furthest, teach us the most, and give us the gift of clarity.

Jenny Holzer, an artist, understands the power and potential of the question. After the events of September 11, 2001, she was contacted by all sorts of people curious to hear how she would memorialize the day. A *New York Times* column written four years later, just as Holzer's tribute *Truisms* was about to be displayed, captured her beautiful response: "Because I didn't really have an answer, I kept thinking about the question."

Getting the Most from *The Answer*

Don't worry about reading *The Answer* in order or all at once. Chances are the first question or questions you flipped to when you took a peek at the book are the questions driving your life now. Those are the questions you want to focus on for the time being. The next step is perspective.

In their book *Glass*, Alan McFarlane and Gerry Martin

highlight Renaissance sculptor and architect Filarete's description of his colleague Filippo Brunelleschi's discovery of the laws of perspective. "If you should desire to represent something in another, easier way," Filarete explained, "take a mirror and hold it up in front of the thing you want to do. Look into it, and you will see the outlines of the thing more easily. . . ."

When life is asking you challenging questions, everything can seem like a blur. Everything you think you know, everything you think you are, everything you think you believe can become so jumbled it is too much for the eye, the heart, and the brain to take in at once. Just as artists, like Filarete, often used mirrors to gain perspective, we can begin to make things clearer by using our questions as a mirror. By looking into, not away from, our questions, the outlines of our answers, and therefore the shape of our lives, will begin to appear.

In Shinto belief, mirrors are standard in shrines because they are meant to reflect a person's true nature. They are not there for us to stare into for narcissistic purposes, but to let us see what's in us with new eyes. In that vision there is power: to know why you're here, what you're here to do, why you are needed, and by whom. These are the things that turn our lives into more than dates of birth and times of death, but unique, irreplaceable masterpieces of being.

In that spirit, think of each chapter in this book as a mirror on the question at hand, offering a new way of approaching and thinking about the question itself. As you begin to see the question differently, you will also start to see how you can become the answer to that question with and through your life. This is where your "highlighter" comes into play.

Your Highlighter

Every single one of us has a built-in highlighter—something that causes you to lean in closer when someone is talking and gives you the chills. It could be a song you suddenly realize you like, or one you haven't heard in a while that you keep playing over and over again, because the words hold new meaning; or a memory you thought you'd forgotten or didn't even remember remembering. It might be someone you're drawn to: perhaps a person who, despite your busy schedule or usual aversion to making the first move when getting to know strangers, has you going the extra mile to create a new relationship; or the discovery of an old friend who you suddenly feel you have more in common with now than you did when you first met. Take note of these things. Write in this book—in the margins, between the lines, anywhere. Take a yellow pad, write your question at the top, and record everything that comes to mind or happens to you that you know has something to do with your emerging answer. And, finally, use the "Your Highlighter" section at the end of each chapter, which includes additional questions to help you locate the answer in you.

Once you've grabbed hold of the question, seen it in a new light, and followed the things that light up sparks inside of you, you'll arrive at—and start to become—the answer to the question life is asking you now.

"I Used to Have to Parallel Park Myself"

This line is from an ad for a deluxe model of a Lexus that claims to parallel park itself. In the ad, the man behind the wheel that moves on its own marvels at the phenomenon in a way that cavemen might have rejoiced at their discovery of fire. I've watched this vehicular miracle tested on two morning talk shows. In each instance, there were embarrassing glitches, and both testers admitted it would have been easier and faster if they had just parked the car themselves.

So when I told my friend Dan about *The Answer* and he said, "What if I'm not equipped to be an answer?" I thought about that car that parks itself. Yes, it may seem that since the car is offering to park for you, you should let it do the parking—just as if people are waiting to offer you "the answers," you should let them answer for you. But you are equipped to take hold of the wheel—your wheel—better. And you're not only equipped, you're obligated—not by me, but by your own life. You know it, in your heart of hearts, in the dark of night, in the moments of truth. You know it. You're here to be an answer in a way that no one else can.

When a reporter from *Time* talked to physicist Max Tegmark, then a theorist at the University of Pennsylvania, about Superstring theory (the existence of multiple universes), Tegmark said, "People have tried very hard to get rid of these multiple universes and failed. They just don't like the concept. They think it's weird. And they're right. But don't we already have good evidence by now that the cosmos really *is* weird?" As the article concludes, "All sorts of universes are possible."

All sorts of universes are possible, which is why a guide with "*the* answers" only gets anyone so far. Eventually, when those answers aren't enough, when you've tried to shove your whole life in one basket and that basket breaks, you can feel like you're breaking, too. But it isn't you. You've just forgotten that the answers are never in one place—that the questions themselves have meaning.

The people who are most successful in the world raise the level of play by arriving at and introducing truths that inspire others. We find ourselves at a point in human history when if we aren't a nation—if not a world—of bar raisers, we'll all lose. And yet, in a time when we need the self-motivation and the freedom to discover our answers to the myriad, complex questions life is asking us, we are looking ever more intensely, if not addictively, to others to do it for us instead. While it's true we will always need leaders, that does not mean that the rest of us are then, by definition, followers. We must all be finders, refiners, and tillers of truths and sources of ideas. A whole universe is one in which every being is a visionary.

While I'm not a guru with a basketful of answers, I can offer you a method for harnessing a power you may not know you already have. That power lies in framing, asking, and using the most important questions we can ask ourselves to transform our lives. I will show you that what you don't know not only *won't* hurt you, but can also actually help you. I will show you that these questions can be your fuel for a more vibrant, more fulfilled day-to-day existence that gives you strength, comfort, momentum, and hope. You'll begin to understand what questions your life *is* an answer to, clearing the path for *your* answers to come from you.

This book won't give you the answers for life, but it

will help you turn your life into an answer—one that is real, authentic, and sustainable for you, by you. And in that, while there are no guarantees, there is peace. You will discover your life's solid ground.

You won't fall off. I promise.

What's to Fear?

I remember when the future was a dream. Now it's, like, a threat.

—Ellie (Naomi Watts) in *Ellie Parker*

"The frightening scene you may see tomorrow and why you should not be scared" was the tease for a local television station's nightly newscast. It made me laugh because the words obviously were meant to frighten me into watching (and I did), even though technically the lead implied there was nothing to fear. As it turned out, the story covered a full-scale siege of the Brooklyn Bridge, replete with tanks and advanced explosive devices, all staged for a movie shoot. But the report commanded my attention and kept me glued, waiting for details.

It doesn't take much to be scared in a twenty-four-hour news, color-coded danger level, "stay tuned for the latest on your security" kind of world with legitimate threats and menacing realities. In fact early twenty-first century living often feels like being home alone, during a storm, in a dark room, amid the violin-shrieking hacker music of the most suspenseful scene from a horror flick, and having someone suddenly tap you on the shoulder. Every five minutes.

As Emily Dickinson titled and made the first line of one of her poems, "One need not be a chamber to be haunted." Nonetheless, even a world at peace would not insulate us from the fears—large and small—that take up residence in our lives. A blank page with a blinking cursor, the loss of a job, a home filled with everything but the voice of the person with whom you once shared it, waiting for a medical test result and wondering how you ever could have taken any day for granted. Every single one of life's peaks is a valley-in-waiting, and every valley is a path to a peak. The only thing we know for certain is that no one knows what's coming next.

No wonder we're fearful. As a friend of mine once said, if we stayed in touch with life's perpetual flux, we would barely be able to get out of bed and tie our shoes in the morning. Out of a certain practical necessity, we invent ways to deal with the fears that are a natural part of living. All too often, though, we learn only one tactic, which is to ignore the fears entirely. We train ourselves to keep aspects of our world in protective lockdown mode and make fallout shelters of our lives. We tell ourselves,

"If I stay where I am, continue doing what I'm doing, and remain very, very quiet (like Elmer Fudd), I won't be afraid." But since Elmer's approach never got him much of anywhere except injured, consider the outcome for those of us who aren't drawn in Technicolor.

In *The Ethics of Ambiguity* philosopher Simone de Beauvoir observed that while no one wants to sense life's inherent dangers, it is precisely because they exist that "words like *victory*, *wisdom*, or *joy* have meaning." "Nothing is decided in advance," she notes, "and it is because man has something to lose and because he can lose that he can also win." Amen to that! The problem is that while de Beauvoir's insight is just the kind of quotation that looks perfect on those motivational office posters you can order from in-flight airline catalogs, somehow it doesn't do the trick when the fear you did not order flies into your life. If being afraid is a necessary ingredient for living, why do we spend so much time trying to dodge it? What's to fear?

If you responded "fear itself," you can thank Franklin Delano Roosevelt. In his perennially meaningful 1933 presidential inaugural address, he urged Americans to understand that they would continue to endure and thrive despite the challenging nature of the times. Roosevelt insisted that a frightening reality would not be the undoing of a nation, but that fear could be. Hence the oft-quoted line, ". . . the only thing we have to fear is fear itself."

Yet few of us have committed to memory the words that followed the phrase we know so well—the ones that somehow fell off of the big billboard of history. When Roosevelt delivered the speech, he continued by defining the "fear itself" as "nameless, unreasoning, unjustified terror, which paralyzes needed efforts to convert retreat into advance." Our thirty-second commander in chief wasn't suggesting that we shouldn't feel fear; he was saying that we shouldn't let a certain kind of fear stop us from moving forward.

Transforming fear into forward motion is an overwhelming human challenge in any age. Every time fear appears, it's easy to think that *this* time, *this* situation is the hardest, most complicated, most troubling, and therefore, the least possible to face. Retreat appears and reappears as a highly attractive option. Four thousand years ago, an Egyptian papyrus—sometimes called "A Man Tired of Life in Dispute with His Soul"—records the struggles of a fraught, nameless individual putting in a request with the universe for, to put it delicately, an early retirement. He receives a less than gentle reply:

> You are hanging up your misery,
> But that Peg,
> it belongs to me!
> Brother,

as long as you burn
you belong to life.

This man's desire to check out of life entirely might be considered extreme, and perhaps today he would get a prescription for Prozac with an Ambien chaser. His fearful reality is like John Milton's description of hell in *Paradise Lost*: "Regions of sorrow, doleful shades, where peace / And rest can never dwell. . . ." However, he could be any one of us in a time when life's fears are their most intense, when something forces us to confront, as Joan Didion calls it in *The Year of Magical Thinking*, "the shallowness of sanity." Fear has the potential to turn life into a boundless battlefield, a war in which survival demands living in a constant state of high alert. But no one can sustain that kind of defensive intensity and still cherish being alive, let alone get anywhere new in the process. However, if fear ceases to be a battle, you can find peace and rootedness and rest again.

From Scared to Sacred

It may not be a coincidence that the distance from "scared" to "sacred" is but two inverted letters. Something singular, unforgettable, and invaluable to the story of our lives is always close at hand if we let being scared be a prelude to a beginning rather than the beginning of the end. The same fears that make you touch sanity's floor with your big toe can also have you walking on some extraordinary ground you never imagined possible— maybe limping ever so slightly, but walking nonetheless. That's exactly what I recall thinking when I heard Felicity Huffman of *Desperate Housewives* fame accept a 2005 Golden Globe award for her performance in the film *Transamerica*. She said, "The second time I didn't work for a year, I gave up any dream of this." What made that line of Huffman's speech so touching was that it gave an important glimmer to the one accessory she wasn't wearing with her stunning gold evening gown: fear—the personal struggles, professional rejections, and plagues of anxiety that easily could have stood between her and that time of her life.

When high-profile people achieve, the fabulously airbrushed magazine photos that come with their "overnight" successes do not capture the 2,022 nights of worry that got them there. That's why the *E! True Hollywood Story* versions of their lives are just as popular as the magazines, if not more. Those portrayals include the triumphs and near-misses in the face of fear that connect us all. Although hard work and perseverance play a crucial role in any headline-grabbing accomplishment, I'm willing to wager the combined value of every piece of red-carpet bling—both loaned and owned—that encounters with great fear play an even more critical role. That's why those walks are not privileges reserved solely for the glitterati. As long as we're willing to keep moving forward when fear offers a cushy couch, when it says the dream we have is a delusion, an infinite number of red carpet strolls await us all.

Achievements born of fear rarely have or require a spotlight. I know talented teachers who've been in the classroom for years and still have the impulse to call in sick on the first day of school; musicians whose entire life's passion is to play to thousands, yet who get so nauseated before a show they forget why they wanted to be there in the first place; relationship counselors who turn into nervous teenagers before dates; priests and rabbis who praise and preach compassion in their communities but hesitate to relate their own suffering. Nonetheless the teachers step into their classrooms and inspire their students, the musicians take the stage and dazzle the crowd, the counselors show up for coffee (and maybe dinner, if things go well), and the spiritual leaders take a risk and trust the people who've put their trust in them.

Stop and take an inventory of the people you admire, and you'll undoubtedly find many among them who taught themselves how to turn "scared" into "sacred."

They spent dark stretches that were likely never seen when you witnessed them at their brightest and made choices without guarantees with the knowledge that they had more life—not less—to create by using fear to move forward. Like Cee-Lo Green of Gnarls Barkley sings in "Crazy," "My heroes had the heart to lose their lives out on a limb."

The ability to move from scared to sacred is not only in your heroes. It's in you. Imagine a different time in your own life, and I'm sure you'll find an example—doesn't matter what or how long ago it was, when you made that move. Place the memory on your mind's mantelpiece as a reminder that you have the ability to develop and live another answer for the fear you're facing now. The details may be different, the stakes higher, your response entirely changed, but the power is there.

If you can't get a visual, think of sperm. Yes, sperm. At the risk of sounding like your high school health teacher (who through some mysterious law of the universe was also your P.E. and driver's ed instructor), these miraculous building blocks of existence tell us a great deal about fear and forward direction. In a January 2007 *New York Times* interview conducted by reporter Claudia Dreifus, Harvard Medical School's Dr. David E. Clapham explained that if human sperm have even the slightest chance of helping create new life they have to swim for at

least fifteen minutes to reach an egg. Then, in strong con-
tradistinction to the nonlaboratory-tested Woody Allen
theory that 90 percent of life is just showing up, these
sperm still have a lot more work to do. Once at the egg, if
they don't hurl themselves at it with a force twenty times
that of the swimming they did to get there in the first
place, the sperm cannot deposit their DNA—meaning,
mission unaccomplished. Clapham almost sounded like he
was describing the Super Friends—Hanna-Barbera's 1970s
team of Superman, Batman, Wonder Woman, and Aqua-
man. "[T]hey crawl long distances in a short period of
time," he raved. "They don't give up until they run out of
energy."

As I read, I wondered if sperm know how improbable
their chances are. What would happen, for instance, if
the realities of this perilous, exacting, and uncertain journey got around the sperm community? Would anyone
ever be born? I realize we're talking about an involuntary
physical process that can be replicated, also rather mirac-
ulously, in a doctor's office. And if you're a guy reading
this, you know that you're probably asleep while all of
that work is taking place. If you're a woman, a man could
be snoring next to you right now. Even so, if this much
implausible determination is an instinctive part of creating a human being—including you—it must also be vital
to the process of being human.

To understand the power to transform fear into forward motion further, let's turn to a different beginning—not of human life, but of the world. In a discussion of how the world came into being, the Zohar, a thirteenth-century text from Spain that is part of a larger Jewish mystical tradition you may know as Kabbalah, explores fear. In that exploration, the mystics place fear into three separate categories. They consider one form "authentic" because it inspires creativity and motion, while the other two are "imposters" whose only function is to impede progress (along the lines of the Roosevelt model).

The mystics argue that the first imposter fear is being afraid that what you already have will disappear, which causes you to put all your effort into preserving the status quo and shielding your possessions. The second pretender to the fear throne is being afraid that you will be ridiculed or punished, which makes you burn out your muscles guarding your image or working almost exclusively to avoid some kind of real or imagined lashing. If neither of these fears is "real," then, what is true fear?

The Zohar advances that fear cannot be deemed genuine unless it holds the power to create a beginning. The text insists that this "sacred fear"—or what a woman in one of my classes exquisitely called "focused fear"—is so invaluable that the world itself would not exist without it.

To emphasize the concept, the mystics daringly reenvision the epic biblical creation kickoff words, "In the beginning God created the heavens and the earth." Instead they write, "With sacred fear God created the heavens and the earth." Their thirteenth-century wisdom has twenty-first-century legs. Choices made from imposter fear produce more imposter fear and keep life at a standstill. But decisions that grow from sacred fear make new worlds.

Your Land of Living

Also writing in the thirteenth century, the Sufi mystic Jalalludin Rumi describes another form of sacred fear and the role it plays in the beginning of new worlds in individual lives. In *The Masnavi*, an ambitious sixty-four-thousand line poem, he teaches:

> The first soul pushes, and your second soul responds, beginning, so don't stay timid. Load the ship and set out. No one knows for certain whether the vessel will sink or reach the harbor. Cautious people say, "I'll do nothing until I can be sure." Merchants know better. If you do nothing, you lose. Don't be one of those merchants who won't risk the ocean!

One of Rumi's translators, Coleman Barks, characterizes this teaching—the idea that one part of the self attempts to push another into creation—as a "necessary dying." He emphasizes Rumi's awareness that while it is human nature to struggle to stay alive, oftentimes we need to let pieces of ourselves fall away in order to live more fully. An exchange between the characters played by Jennifer Beals (Bette) and Marlee Matlin (Jodi) on the Showtime series *the L word* sharpens the concept. Bette and Jodi are falling in love, but Bette is particularly frightened, still stalled nearly two years after the breakup of an eight-year relationship. Jodi tells Bette that when something scares her, the more she feels like she could "die" doing it, the more she knows it's worth doing. Bette says, "I don't want to die right now." Jodi responds, "Neither do I."

While our anonymous friend from ancient Egypt desired death, what he really wanted was to avoid living through the frightening "necessary dying" that Rumi depicts and *the L word* scene encapsulates, even though this "necessary dying" yields more life. Whether it occurs, however, is in our hands. Although being scared gets us thinking the opposite, the choice is always there. We can use everything we have to retreat, or we can use all that we are to move forward.

Another way to think of the "retreat" approach is the

classic expression "burying your head in the sand." Inter-
estingly, though, this phrase stems from a myth about the
ostrich. In fact, an ostrich does not bury its head in the
sand when fearful. What it does is more tragic. When
this bird senses a threat, it does bring its head low to the
ground, but it doesn't dig—it simply rubs its face in the
dirt. What I find odd about this behavior is that it doesn't
just involve avoiding the fear, but being too afraid to avoid
avoiding it. What's even more bizarre is that an ostrich can
be ten feet tall, weigh nearly four hundred pounds, and
have the power to run forty miles an hour on legs strong
enough to kick a lion to death. Why, then, don't we associate the ostrich with these attributes? Why is it known for
what it doesn't do, rather than for what it can? And so as
not to unfairly dis the ostrich, let's ask the same of ourselves. If someone coined a phrase from your life when it
came to facing fear, what would you want the saying to be?

While you're thinking, consider this: human brains
are the largest and best developed among mammals—
particularly in the cerebral cortex where problem solv-
ing occurs (probably why you can be multitasking right
now)—yet no one knows for sure how much of our
brain's capacity we use or might be capable of using.
Albert Brooks's film *Defending Your Life* offers a decid-
edly unscientific, yet compelling, clue to the mystery. In

Brooks's cinema universe, the first stop in the hereafter is a place called Judgment City, where everyone gets a thorough life review, the ultimate litmus test of which is how courageous he or she was while on earth. The resident defenders and prosecutors of Judgment City who conduct these reviews are also human beings, but ones with advanced degrees—not in law, but in the use of their brains. Brooks's attorney, played by Rip Torn, claims to use 48 percent of his, while "regular" people use a mere three. The marked difference in capacity, he says, is fear.

Perhaps that is what "clear thinking" really is—not allowing fear to rule your mind, your thoughts, your decisions; seeing fear as part of life, not apart from life. We see this idea in motion in a verse from Psalm 142, when a man brought low by fear says, nonetheless, his "portion is in the land of the living." Imagine if this psalmist and the anonymous man from ancient Egypt who was told, rather unceremoniously, that he "belonged to life" had been able to talk to each other, if they had been able to hear Roosevelt's words. We have the gift of all of their wisdom and their struggles to remind us that while we may belong to the land of the living, our lives needn't belong to the "nameless, unreasoning, unjustified terror which paralyzes needed efforts to convert retreat into advance."

Your portion is in the land of the living, but you must

find your wisdom to claim and shape it. Even if it's not your preference, or mine, long before we entered the world, the decision was rendered that fear is an essential ingredient in being alive. However, if "What's to Fear?" is a question driving your life now, you can decide what *kind* of fear you want to be part of your answer. Will you give "imposter fear" the authority, allowing it to keep you stuck in a nonevent, like "The frightening scene you may see tomorrow and why you should not be scared"? Or will you find what's sacred in the fear and use it to guide your next steps? Although the feelings that accompany the "imposter" and "sacred" elements of your fear all have power, by identifying the elements that are life-generating, as opposed to paralysis-inducing, you will have a power you can activate to move forward.

Y O U R   H I G H L I G H T E R

Remember, you have your own personal highlighter. It will help lead you to the ways you can be the answer to this question in your life. Your highlighter might make you more aware of a lyric in a song, draw your attention to an old photo you pass a million times in your house each day but rarely notice, make your eyes open wider when someone utters a particular phrase, or have you shedding tears at a scene from a movie (even if it's a comedy!). Whatever it may be, your highlighter is lighting up the answer forming inside you. These additional questions are here to help your highlighter engage.

- For you, right now, what's to fear? What is the biggest thing that gives you the "Wouldn't it be easier to call in sick?" feeling?

- In what ways is it an imposter, or paralysis-inducing, fear?

- In what ways is it a sacred, life-generating fear?

- How can you use the life-generating element of the fear?

- What does your world look like when you imagine you do use that life-generating element of your fear?

Am I Good?

The web of our life is of a mingled yarn, good and ill together.

—Shakespeare, *All's Well That Ends Well*

Do you believe in your life?

Do you believe that if every unattractive, downright abominable thing about you were to be revealed to the whole world—posters plastered on buses, signs trailing from prop planes buzzing over crowded beaches, words bloated with private information crawling across the bottom of strangers' flat screens—you would be good?

Could you still see yourself as good—in that Alanis Morissette "That I Would Be Good" sort of way—if you gained a few (or ten) pounds, if you went into debt, if a critic said your best days were waving you a "na-na-na-na-hey-hey"–style good-bye? What about then?

Before I get out of bed each morning, before I even sit

up, I utter a blessing that I've inherited from my tradition: "I am grateful to You, living Sovereign, for returning my soul to me with compassion. Your faith is unbounded." I am perpetually awed that my ancestors fashioned such an audacious prayer. Religious contexts, including my own, repeatedly focus on people putting their faith in higher powers. But higher powers putting faith in you? Or, as I understand it, a universe that puts its trust in you at the start of every day, that counts on you—no matter what happened the day before or what may happen in the immediate twenty-four hours to come? That is an exquisite, complex, yet hopeful responsibility to shape the world's life with your own in any and every eventuality.

So if something as big as the universe can believe in us, why can it be so hard for us to believe in ourselves?

That is, after all, what we're really facing when "Am I Good?" is the question driving our lives. Like those iconic Russian *matryoshka* nesting dolls, this question has other questions nestled inside of it: Do I deserve this (whether the "this" is something you've always wanted or something you've dreaded)? Is the person or are the people saying I'm "no good" right? Is an experience I'm having now compelling me to view myself in a way I never thought I would, and do I like—or even recognize—what I see? And if I don't, can I change the picture?

As liberating as it may be to see each day as a new

opportunity, if it's glimpsed solely through someone else's eyes fixed disapprovingly on us, a new day can be little more than an audition with a menacing array of real and imagined opportunities to fail. In this sense you don't have to be a dancer to relate to the character Paul's inner dialogue from the Broadway musical *A Chorus Line*, sung while he steps, kicks, leaps, and pivots through a grueling cattle call: "Who am I anyway? . . . What should I try to be?" You're practically guaranteed to fall if you're dancing as fast as you can to this sort of internal soundtrack just to stay one step ahead of hearing, "You're fired!"

Even if you never sharpen your elbows to compete for a job as The Donald's "Apprentice" or your knives for the title of "Top Chef"; even if Randy, Paula, and Simon never hear your dazzling, shower-perfected rendition of "I'm Every Woman," when "Am I Good?" is little more than an understudy for saying you're bad, as Shakespeare wrote in *As You Like It*, "All the world's a stage, and all the men and women merely players." Hearing the question that way allows for a mere handful of roles for you to play in life: winner or loser, hero or villain. No in-between.

In a culture of YouTubed public plummets with fashion and design "police" and reality shows with judges who achieve their oddly powerful status as randomly as their willing "defendants," we've become confused. For all the pervasive talk of good and evil as we stand in the

foyer of the twenty-first century, we're no closer to understanding or defining either term, except in the rather con-
spicuous cases of genocidal, diabolical dictators—past
and present—and terrorists who thankfully still comprise
a minority, albeit a terrible one, of the human race. We're
not confused about them, but those of us who don't fall
into the aforementioned categories can have a difficult
time distinguishing between the value of our lives and
some rather narrow notions of goodness. Because life is
so much more complex than we'd prefer, and people—
including ourselves—far more difficult to typecast than
we'd like, we often resort to a limited set of descriptors in
the hopes that it will soothe us, when, in fact, its detach-
ment from reality only makes things harder.

Before you dismiss this as a statement of relativism in a
society many would argue doesn't have enough standards,
take a moment to assess how snacking on people's frailties
and foibles has arguably surpassed baseball as our national
pastime. Think about how many hours of television cover-
age and gallons of ink are devoted to the dissection of public
figures' personal lives—whom they date, marry; how they
parent; what they eat, say, drink; how they spend money.
And most of that attention consists of unsolicited advice
offered by scores of "experts" who've never met the people in
question so much as once, capturing people at their absolute
worst, trapping them in lows that aren't just frozen in time,

but stuck on a continuous, unforgiving loop. To quote U2, "Is it getting better?" Are we really so much better off, collectively or individually, for our attempts to stuff life—and more often the lives of others—into two carry-on-sized bags (no liquids, please!): one marked "Good" and the other "Bad" (or "Evil")? Is there less pain and suffering, a more equitable distribution of resources, greater equality, tranquility, and an overall sunnier sense of well-being when we limit everything to those two containers? Do we benefit from more inspired leadership, enjoy stronger relationships, find there is less covering up, and a greater number of positive revelations? Or are the revelations that consume much of our time and attention not revelations but condemnations, most of which amount to shameful, sensationalistic tale-bearing that tells the same tale over and over: people are imperfect. They've got it together and they unravel; they rise to the occasion and they topple over it. As Chris Matthews asks panels of political insiders from his weekly Sunday television pulpit, "Tell me something I don't know." How about this: unless you reside alone in a cave, standards and categories, including those of "good" and "bad," are a necessary fact of living. They do not, however, hold or determine the final answer to the unpredictable arc of any life. They do not have the last word as to whether you or I or anyone is good.

Thomas Jefferson, a deeply religious man who famously

inspired the separation between church and state in America, was influenced and inspired by English political philosopher John Locke. Jefferson was known to quote from Locke's 1689 "A Letter Concerning Toleration," in which Locke said, "The care, therefore, of every man's soul belongs unto himself and is to be left unto himself." Writing in the same century as Jefferson on another side of the ocean, a Lithuanian-born rabbi named Israel Salanter spearheaded an ethics-based movement with his own personal mantra, one strikingly similar to the line that had resonated with one of our founding fathers. Salanter claimed, "A pious Jew is not one who worries about his fellow man's soul and his own stomach; a pious Jew worries about his own soul and his fellow man's stomach." Because *soul*, like *good* and *evil*, is an oft used and underdefined term, think of it as another way of saying "life." This is one of the first things I learned in rabbinical school. A word in the Bible most frequently translated as "soul" in English actually can mean "neck" or "throat." If that place is blocked or constricted we cannot breathe, and therefore we cannot live.

When you take a deep breath, you know that you'll have to let it out if you want to keep living. Exhale and eventually you'll need to draw breath again for the same reason. As such, there is no separation in the most basic act of living: the inhale is inextricably linked to the exhale and vice versa. And so it is with our attempts to polarize the good and the bad in life and in ourselves.

That is what both Jefferson and Salanter were saying: that we own the rights to the value and character of our own lives, but that we have not been endowed with the inalienable right to judge those of others. They understood that for those of us who live in the real world (not the reality show, but among other human beings who have done more than sign a waiver with MTV), we do choose, by dint of our citizenship or membership in a particular community, to adhere to certain laws and standards that define good and bad for the sake of order, public safety, and clarity of boundaries. They knew that compliance with these categories is a precondition of belonging, but that it should not be mistaken for an overarching or exhaustive definition of human goodness. Or, as the Roman philosopher Seneca explained in his treatise "On Anger": "What a narrow innocence it is to be good only according to the law." An excellent point, given that neither the realms of government nor religion themselves, in which categories of good and bad are legislated and defined, are the final arbiter of what is good. We have witnessed, and continue to witness, moments throughout history when that which has been deemed right or good according to law has later been labeled injurious, oppressive, and unjust to entire groups and individuals alike, forcing necessary, often dreadfully slow, change. But leaving open the question of what is, in fact, good always leaves a window for improvement. That window is crucial, whether it comes to the improvement of a self or a society. For, as Seneca is also noted for having observed, "Bad is the plan that can never be changed."

Inarguably, categories of all types grant our lives important structures and meanings. But the ever-unfolding mystery of each human life—the struggle to understand ourselves, our actions, how we develop and change, who we are, and who we might be under a variety of circumstances—exists apart from the Declaration of Independence or any organized form of religion, and will endure as long as people do on this earth. That mystery prevents any completely honest life story from ever being written using only one word, whether that word is *good* or *bad*.

This is not relativistic, but realistic. The shared story of humankind is that we are surrounded by inspirational, hardworking, visionary, generous, strong, well-intentioned people with whom we agree and with whom we do not. But look carefully, get to know any of them well enough, and you will find imperfections in them all. In fact the better you know most anyone, the harder it is to stuff them in the "good" or the "bad" bag. Because we never know exactly what we would do or whom we would be in anyone else's life but our own, and through our connections to others—often most notably with those we thought we had pegged for being our exact opposite—we realize how easily the details of their lives could be ours. This being the case, imagine how much more energy we might have to devote to having a positive impact on the world if we were to follow the teaching of Francois-Marie Arouet, better known as Voltaire. "We are all full of weakness and errors," he said in his essay, "A Plea for Tolerance and Reason." "Let us mutually pardon each other our follies—it is the first law of nature."

Years ago I officiated at a ritual for the naming of a baby girl, a child's first official welcome into the community and into the world. As I was leaving, the baby's mother handed me a book called *Messages from Amma: In the Language of the Heart*. She told me that it had inspired her, so much so that she had used the book itself as a focal point during her labor and delivery. I would later discover that the work contains the translated wisdom of an Indian holy woman who does staggering international humanitarian work creating and providing networks of care for orphans, the elderly, and the impoverished. Before I did my homework about Amma, though, I figured that anything powerful enough to get a woman through childbirth without drugs was worth attention. As the spine creaked on the brand-new book I'd been given, it practically opened on its own to the page with this teaching: "Your third eye will never open if, in the name of spirituality, you close your eyes to the world. Spiritual realization is the ability to see yourself in all beings, to look through the third eye while keeping your other two eyes wide open."

Eastern religions identify the third eye as one of the body's energy centers, or chakras. While not an actual physical eye, it is linked to the way we see the world. Located in the center of the brow, it occupies the meridian between the left and right hemispheres of the brain. It enables us to see the whole picture, to take in all of the "in-betweens," the gray: the things that cannot be shoved into one bag or another.

Many artists credit Renaissance master Leonardo da Vinci with saying, "A gray day provides the best light." Since most of our days are spent in the gray, the sooner we learn how to use their light, the more skilled we'll be at painting the most authentic portrait of who we are and who we want to be.

Part of believing in your own life is claiming "Am I Good?" as your question not from a defensive stance, not because someone might say you're bad, but because you're willing to look at everything you'll see by letting your life do the asking.

I'm No Angel

"I'm No Angel" is more than a late-eighties Gregg All-man tune. It could be the anthem for humanity, perhaps one that would have had certain Talmudic scholars waving lighters at a crowded stadium concert if they were to hear it today. Ancient lore records a sibling rivalry of sorts between angels and human beings, with the former lobbying against the creation of humanity at all. They try to tell God that human beings will only screw up the universe, running amok through God's brand-spanking-new world like children with muddy boots. Instead of taking their advice, though, God sets fire to every angel focus group that is antihuman. It seems that the Deity was looking for some yes-cherubs to support this particular project, and after a couple of tries a third group of angels finally got wise. In the face of God's rhetorical question as to whether or not humanity should exist they gave the only answer that could help them save themselves, even though they were not onboard with the idea: yes.

The first chance the angels get to offer an "I told you so," however, they do. When God looks more than slightly askance at humanity in the age of Noah, clearly having second thoughts about the whole human enterprise, the angels are right there saying that the first two focus groups had it right all along. But even then, according to this rabbinic soap opera, God says, Jackson Five–style, "No matter what they do, I'll be there." Or, as Bengali author Rabindranath Tagore wrote in his poem "Stray Birds," "Every child comes with the message that God is not yet discouraged of man." In any event, God refuses to abandon humanity. And so the angels, the Eddie Haskells and Nellie Olesons from on high, are foiled again.

Meanwhile back at the Bible, the apostle Peter's observation in the Book of Acts takes on a different meaning when he says, "I now see how true it is that God has no favorites." The angels want to be God's favorite, but to no avail. And among human beings, despite all appearances, there are no "fortunate sons," either. For, in the words of Ecclesiastes, ". . . the race is not to the swift, nor the battle to the strong, nor bread to the wise, nor riches to the visionaries, and not favor for the learned; time and chance happen to them all."

From generation to generation of imperfect human beings, most of whom suffer and succeed, few of whom travel an entirely linear, smooth, pothole-free route through life, everyone gets a fair shot to make something of his life even though life is anything but fair. Despite the angels' arguments to the contrary, and perhaps those of some humans, our imperfections are not a sign of the world's incremental descent into some vile oblivion, but a challenge to our capacity to keep climbing to new heights with the flaws in tow. If you need to be a "fortunate son" to be good, if you need to be the only one who gets the gold star, then "Am I Good?" may not be your question. You may not be struggling with being good, but with looking good. There is a difference.

South African president and former political prisoner Nelson Mandela's struggles and suffering for the betterment of humanity are well known, yet his frailties and foibles are similarly revealed, often by his own admission. As he said in his 1994 inaugural address, "I am not a saint, unless you think of a saint as a sinner who keeps on trying." Mandela's words evoke the heart of a teaching from another time and another part of the globe. Bodhisattva Amitabha, a Buddha whose wisdom is the foundation for the Pure Land Chinese school of Buddhism that emerged in the fifth century, made a bold statement when he included this among his forty-eight vows for attaining ultimate bliss: "If all men save deadly sinners may not enter it, I will not enter Buddhahood." If asking yourself if you're good becomes a pageant in which you imagine a singular salutary crown awaiting only one person, the question isn't driving your life. It's hijacking it.

Showing What You're Made Of

You don't have to prove to the angels or to any other humans that you deserve to be here. You already are. The question is *how* do you want to be here? How do you turn "Am I Good?" into something you can answer with your life that won't leave you feeling perpetually vulnerable to the inevitable passing judgments of others, simply stranded in the same moment over and over again, or left outside an exclusive club? First, you have to take a brave look at what you're made of, and it's not all pretty. As another Buddhist text, the Dhammapada, advises, "One may conquer a million men in a single battle; however, the greatest and best warrior conquers himself."

You already know that you're no angel. That means you have a body; you sleep, eat, drink, earn money, and have sex. Not all at once, but you get the idea. The eleventh-century Moslem theologian Abu Hamid Muhammad Ibn Muhammad Al-Ghazali listed the ingredients this way in *The Main Problems of Abu Nasr Al-Paraba*:

> Man's nature is made up of four elements, which produce in him four attributes, namely, the beastly, the brutal, the satanic, and the divine. In man there is something of the pig, the dog, the devil, and the saint.

In any context, you and I are combination platters of desires, instincts, inclinations, and sensibilities, all of which change for reasons both beyond and within our control. Some might say, then, that the only way to be good is to cut out the bad. But that is sort of like when the USDA changed the food pyramid, and told us to cut out all the fat in our diets. This begat the "Snackwells Era," during which everything was fat-free, and it was good. But people didn't get healthier or thinner, and before we knew it we had entered the "Age of Atkins." It was all fat, all the time, and it, too, was good. Until we realized we needed some whole-grain carbohydrates with our three-egg, rib-eye omelet breakfasts if we wanted to keep our original kidneys. Today, the USDA has twelve different food pyramids, listed under the heading "My Pyramid," which take into account fluctuations in age, physical activity, and weight, among other things. And the diet book wars rage on, bringing us to an awareness as great, yet as simple, as sliced (sprouted-grain) bread: with so many variables in play, what's good for one person may not be good for another. Do you know what's good for you?

Dr. Wangari Maathai, the first African woman and the first environmentalist ever to receive the Nobel Peace Prize, founded the Green Belt Movement in 1977. The Kenya-based Green Belt Movement is now an international agent for social and ecological change, women's

economic sustainability, and peaceful governmental practices. Maathai relates how she "stumbled and fell" in what
she calls her search for "the good," in a 1991 interview
with Priscilla Sears from the journal *In Context*:

> [O]thers told me that I shouldn't have a career, that I
> shouldn't raise my voice, that women are supposed to
> have a master. . . . Finally I was able to see that if I had
> a contribution I wanted to make, I must do it, despite
> what others said.

If Maathai had let "Am I Good?" control her life based
solely on what she had been told to believe was good,
many of her current and future contributions so easily
could have been wasted. Her struggle to get the question
into her own control by searching herself, her willingness
to let the totality of her life be an answer to that question,
has made a difference in the lives of countless others.

We are not all here to win Nobel Peace Prizes or found
international movements, although we could be. Who
knows? However, none of us has a clue until we're willing
to risk losing the "good" label, until we're willing to face
ourselves as a whole in order to do good, to let the con-
tents take precedence over the packaging. In this sense
you can hear echoes of Alexander Pope's poem, "Know
Thyself," in Maathai's story, when he says that human

beings are "created half to rise and half to fall." Maathai's path of ups-and-downs with the "good" question also bears the footprints of Trappist monk Thomas Merton's wisdom I once heard quoted in my interfaith study group: "We stumble and fall constantly even when we are most enlightened. But when we are in true spiritual darkness, we do not even know that we have fallen."

The twelfth-century philosopher Moses Maimonides held in a work called the *Shemoneh Perakim* that "it is an indisputable fact that all a human being's deeds are dependent upon him. If he so wishes, he does, and if he so wishes, he doesn't do. And he is not forced in this." Being free to stumble, fall, and rise, then, is no easy feat. In that sense, and with all due respect to Janis Joplin, freedom is not another word for nothing left to lose. In fact, there's quite a lot at stake.

Stumbling is a particularly unattractive risk, especially if you pride yourself on never so much as tripping. After all, if you stumble you might fall and never get back up. Then again if you don't fall, you may never know just how tall you might have been able to stand in your life having dusted yourself off and stretched to your feet again. Getting to what you believe is your lowest may be the prelude to rising to previously unfathomable heights. As I once heard a TV market analyst say, when a stock is low, the slightest mention of good news can send it soaring 300 percent in value. In this sense, asking if you're good can be that news. If you let the question work for you, it can signal the beginning of a change that will lead you to value and trust your life and its possibilities more.

A Muslim and Jewish tradition put this notion into strikingly similar terms. In the Mishkat-ul-Masabih of Waliuddin Abu Abdullah Mahmud Al-Tabrizi, the "slightest good news" is making the tiniest move toward change:

> Allah, Most High, says: He who approaches near to me one span, I will approach to him one cubit; and he who approaches near to me one cubit, I will approach near to him one fathom; and whoever approaches me walking, I will come to him running. . . .

Rabbi Yassa, in an ancient commentary called *Shir Ha'Shirim Rabbah*, imagines a God inviting people to reveal an openness to change "no bigger than the eye of a needle." In so doing, that tiny portal will be widened "into openings through which wagons and carriages can pass."

Determining what that opening is for you can turn this question into a beginning, rather than the setup for an immutable, one-word judgment that can only leave you stalled in the midst of a potentially full and fruitful life in progress.

Practice, Practice, Practice

Perhaps you're wondering if you're good because you're angry—with someone or something: with an outcome of a relationship, a professional endeavor, or your general state of being. Then your approach to finding your answer begins with identifying the source of the anger. As Aristotle instructed in his *Nicomachean Ethics*:

> Anybody can become angry—that is easy, but to be angry with the right person and to the right degree and at the right time and for the right purpose, and in the right way—that is not within everybody's power and is not easy.

There is no way to live and never be angry. Human beings get angry, are even motivated by anger to achieve and try harder. But lingering anger eventually turns us on ourselves, or worse, on people or situations where it no longer fits the program and may even threaten to destroy what we care about most. That ill-fitting anger can leave you no choice but to feel no good. In those moments, as Don Henley sings, "it's about forgiveness."

Forgiveness takes practice, mostly because it's the part that's our choice. The things that happen to precipitate the need for forgiveness oftentimes are not, and it's so much easier to think we're making ourselves good by feeling right—and righteous—in our indignation. The only problem is all that time we spend telling ourselves how good we are for being the wronged party, we're avoiding our own part in the story. Even when we have been genuinely wronged, truly victimized, we remain responsible for how and if we proceed, with what attitude, and whether we do so with wisdom, power, strength, and purpose.

Walking down the street one day, I overheard a little girl recount the details of a play date gone bad to her mother. The specifics were remarkably well-archived and compelling in their vivid narration coming from a child who couldn't have been more than seven.

"But that was two years ago," her mother said.

"Well," the little girl said to her mom, "I can't stop my memory." With that, they both stopped, right there on Amsterdam Avenue, somewhere between Seventy-fifth and Seventy-sixth Street, and so did I, to continue to eavesdrop.

"True," the mom replied. "But you can forgive."

We can't go back and rewrite the moments that have contributed to the anger we've stored, but no one's going to hear our case and award damages, no less the reigning title of "Truly Wronged Human," regardless of how compellingly we tell the tale. The memories are always there and may even stir up rather live feelings we thought had abated. But without remembering to forgive, there is nowhere for the anger, frustration, and hurt to go. And suddenly we're those angels, sitting on high, not really a part of life, holding grudges that have no weight in the universe—just hurting ourselves.

In *The History of Love*, a novel by Nicole Krauss, the main character—now an elderly man—speaks of what can happen when we don't forgive and describes his own struggle to develop the practice:

> I want to say somewhere: I've tried to be forgiving. And yet. There were times in my life, whole years, when anger got the better of me. Ugliness turned me inside out. There was a certain satisfaction in bitterness. I courted it. It was standing outside, and I invited it in. I scowled at the world. And the world scowled back. We were locked in a stare of mutual disgust. . . . And then one day I realized . . . I wasn't really angry. Not anymore. I had left my anger somewhere long ago. Put it down on a park bench and walked away. And yet. It had been so long. I didn't know any other way of being. One day I woke up and said to myself: *It's not too late.* The first days were strange. I had to practice smiling in front of the mirror. But it came back to me. It was as if a weight had been lifted. I let go, and something let go of me.

If the person you're having the hardest time forgiving is yourself, you also need to locate the source of your anger and disappointment. What is happening in your life to make you ask whether you're good? And before you squeeze your eyes closed to whatever the elements are that you're trying to make go away because they don't fit the frame—or so you thought—before you turn your focus to someone else you can blame and get yourself off the hook, someone who can bear the brunt of your inability to accept your own shortcomings, get those elements in your control by seeing them as the parts of you that exist to help you change. And then ask yourself if you can risk ignoring them; if your life is in greater peril for looking through them, not at them; if the day has come, in the spirit of these words attributed to French diarist Anaïs Nin, "when the risk to remain tight in a bud [is] more painful than the risk it [takes] to blossom."

A Very Good Year

So, you're ready to risk taking a good, long look with "Am I Good?" For the shift you need to find your answer to this question, we'll turn to the Chairman of the Board. Not God, but Frank Sinatra. Sinatra put "It Was a Very Good Year" on the charts some four decades ago, singing about the different phases of his life (with accompanying romances, of course). The last verse demonstrates how

"Am I Good?" can be a question that expands who and how you are in the world. And so I yield to the Chairman: "And now I think of my life as vintage wine, from fine old kegs, from the brim to the dregs."

Valuing the brim to the dregs and everything in between makes "Am I Good?" a question that will guide you to an effective, positive, honest answer that you, quite literally, can live with. While obviously this question is no laughing matter, I'll use a frequent opener to many a joke to reframe it for precisely that purpose: I've got good news and I've got bad news.

The bad news is that if you want to know definitively that you're good, you'll have to wait to be certain. It may be something you can only see when you look in the rearview mirror at your life—glimpsing more than one episode, one action, or even a handful of years. The world may call you good when you're gone or it may remain silent on the matter, and neither may be deserved. And if you believe in a higher power or life after death, you'll be taking it up with the real Chairman (or -woman) of the Board, and find out once and for all if there is a final accounting. In any event, spending your life waiting to be called good keeps you from all the facets of living that can lead to doing the good that you can.

Which brings me to the good news. You are, in this moment, without a doubt, *very* good. You may be wondering how it's possible to be very good without being good. Isn't that sort of like skipping a grade? In Saint Augustine's *Confessions of a Sinner*, he comments on the Bible's account of the world's creation. Speaking to God, he notes:

> In the case of each of your works you first commanded them to be made, and when they had been made you looked at each in turn and saw that it was good. I have counted and found that Scripture tells us seven times that you saw that what you had made was good, and when you looked for the eighth time and saw the whole of your creation, we are told that you found it not only good but very good, for you saw all at once as one whole. Each separate work was good, but when they were all seen as one, they were not merely good: they were very good.

Saint Augustine's observation from the fourth century CE (AD) that the "very good" encompasses the totality of all creation, that "very good" is the sum of all of its parts, reminded me of a teaching attributed to Rabbi Shmuel bar Nachman two centuries later in a text called *Genesis Rabbah*. In it he contends that the repeated phrase "Behold, it was good" in Genesis refers to the impulse to good, while the pronouncement following the birth of humanity (coinciding with the culmination of all the work)—"Behold, it was very good"—refers to the impulse to bad, or evil. As Rabbi Shmuel continues, "Scripture teaches that were it not for the impulse to evil, a man would not build a house, take a wife, have children, or do business. As [it is written in Ecclesiastes]: I have also noted that all labor and skillful enterprise come from men's envy of each other." In both men's eyes, the "very good" is the everything of life that, on some profound level, renders the stark dichotomization of "good" and "bad" a false goal. There is no "good" and "bad," just "very good," in the sense that if we begin to eliminate the so-called "good" from the so-called "bad" we have no sense of what we'll unravel, halt, or destroy— things that in their totality aren't only better for us, but help us make a better world.

If you could delete the scenes from your life when you've felt the lowest, the worst, the deepest sense of disappointment in yourself, can you say you would still be who you are, or more specifically, that you would be the person you've become and like now without them? Think of a situation that brought out your best—unearthed more from undiscovered coffers in your soul. Would you have called it good at the time? Could you have gotten there without first having made the "wrong" choices, worked the "wrong" job, been in the "wrong" relationship? Would you know how to live the way you live, love the way you love, do what you do?

If your question is "Am I Good?" you're probably concerned about the fact that you're very good. You're probably at a point where who you want or know yourself to be is in conflict with an experience or personal revelation that, in fact, may be precisely what it takes to get you there, but that doesn't look or feel attractive in this instant. It may be a small discovery; it could be the biggest personal archaeological site you've stumbled upon in your life, complete with gritty potsherds and fragments you'll have to pick up if you want to get to the top of things. But even as you locate your very good, your mixture and totality, everything doesn't have to fall apart. You can still possess an ideal and acknowledge how and where you're falling short of it by holding the hope that you may be even better than you ever could have been for having done so in the first place—that you, like the creation of the world, are becoming more complete, not less, the more complex the picture becomes. That you can face it all and still rise to greet another day believing in your life, praying, to paraphrase one of the many pieces of wisdom passed down from pitching legend Satchel Paige, when it rains *and* when the sun is shining.

Because the "very good" does not depend upon absolutes, on status or stasis, or on one particular set of conditions, but on an ongoing mastery of all that you are made of; because it includes and accounts for every set of eventualities we can imagine and all the surprises we cannot, you can set aside the worry as to whether you are good and be in a constant state of working toward doing good with everything you are. In sickness and in health, for richer or for poorer, in scandal and in celebration.

As the Dalai Lama instructs in *The Dalai Lama's Book of Wisdom*, "With realization of one's potential and self-confidence in one's ability, one can build a better world." Potential usually carries a positive valence. But potential is merely an expression of possibility, and possibilities are varied. However, if you realize your full potential, namely the range of inclinations that you possess, and learn how to live with all of them, no matter what happens in your life, your life has the best chance of positively affecting those of others and, on a larger scale, the world. You won't be perfect. You will cause pain at times and you will surely experience it. There will be things you'll never be able to take back or erase. The choice is yours: live fully—even when the picture gets complicated—and make good come from it, or live carefully to be good and trade the label for all the good you could do.

I don't say this lightly. Because we don't live in isolation, our mistakes, and therefore our "very goodness," rarely only affect us. They can close doors we've worked years to open—in work, reputation, love, and friendship. In Bernard Malamud's story "The Magic Barrel," Leo

Finkle, a rabbinical student in his sixth and final year of training confronts his own "very good." He has been told that he'll better his chances for gainful employment if he marries. So he employs a matchmaker to find him a bride. On his first arranged date, Leo realizes that the woman with whom he is taking a seemingly benign stroll through the park has already fallen in love with the "semi-mystical Wonder Rabbi" the matchmaker has painted him to be. As she asks typical get-to-know-you questions, he makes the acquaintance of an unwelcome awareness: he doesn't fit the description by a long shot. When the date ends, his date with himself is just beginning. This is Malamud's account of Leo's blind date with the very good:

> The week that followed was the worst of his life. . . . He seriously considered leaving the Yeshiva, although he was deeply troubled at the thought of the loss of all his years of study—saw them like pages torn from a book, strewn over the city—and at the devastating effect of this decision upon his parents. But he had lived without knowledge of himself, and never in the Five Books and all the Commentaries—mea culpa—had the truth been revealed to him. He did not know where to turn. . . . But gradually, as the long and terrible week drew to a close, he regained his composure and some idea of purpose in life: to go on as planned. Although he was imperfect, the ideal was not.

Six years of school. Six years of study and dedication on the verge of being torn from Leo's life story because he wasn't quite as "good" as he'd hoped he already was. But Leo's ability to face the very good in his life reminds him of how much he values his ideal image of what it means to be the kind of rabbi, person, and teacher he thought he already was. He sees where he is from all angles—he isn't who he thought he was, he doesn't have the answers he thought he did. He falls apart and it is in the breaking that he sees clearly what he wants and where he wants to be. He faces the everything and lives to write the tale with the rest of his days. And were the story to go on, no doubt we'd find Leo facing the everything again.

We tend to think that once we've made a discovery, implemented a change, that we can go on autopilot—that coordinates entered into the onboard navigational system will remain there forever. But as I learned in a book called *The Quotable Soul*, a German-American author by the name of Max C. Otto once said, redemption is "not an instantaneous deed, but a lifelong adventure." Singer Judy Collins has brought this into stark relief when speaking publicly about her own daily struggles to transform hard-won wisdom into daily action, using skills carved from her own everything: her tragedies, her stumbling blocks, her talents, her happiness, and her sorrow. When Collins brings her famously calm and clear voice to that most famous version of Joni Mitchell's "Both Sides Now," she sings, "But something's lost but something's gained in living every day." These words are more than lyrics for a woman who became an advocate for suicide prevention after her son took his life, who faces her own lifelong battle with depression every day with exercise, work, love, constantly learning and relearning how to live. Collins, the soothing voice for generations on many a record player, CD, and iPod, the strong voice for social change, has seen it all from both sides. She knows the very good.

So now it's your turn. Find the "very good" in your life at this moment—all the elements that are at play. Put it next to the ideal you're trying to live toward. What aspects are helping get you there, and what aspects are pushing you further away? Ask yourself if the ideal remains one that you want to coordinate your life to reach, even if you may spend your whole life trying to grow into it. If the ideal has changed for you, you are being challenged to embrace a new one, and must shift coordinates accordingly. This alone could be the source of your discomfort and the reason this question has entered your life. By re-embracing an ideal or discovering the new one you are headed toward, you will feel good again.

Y O U R   H I G H L I G H T E R

As you're taking hold of this question and moving toward your answers, remember that you'll guide yourself to them by letting your internal highlighter do some of the work. You may recall something someone said long ago that springs to mind because you're ready to hear it. You could be drawn to a piece of art, the language of a recipe, or an article in a magazine that you may agree or disagree with—in either case, both are helpful compasses to help lead you to what you know to be true on your insides now. These questions, drawn from themes in the chapter, are also here to make "Am I Good?" a driving force, rather than a stumbling block, in your life:

- Is the question primarily coming from you or from outside of you?

- If it is coming from you, what ideal is being challenged?

- Does the ideal need a course correction (i.e., is it an ideal you no longer are striving to achieve) or do you need to examine how the components of your life now are getting you closer to or further away from an ideal you continue to value?

- If the question is coming from outside of you, how much authority do you want to give it?

- Is the question making you more of who you could be, or is it keeping you from growing?

- Is the question compelling you to be "very good"—to see parts of yourself you may be surprised to see? If so, what are those parts and how might they fit into who you are and want to be so that you are better equipped to do good for yourself and do your best for others?

- Is the question calling you to change?

- If so, what part of that change do you know you can't afford to ignore—no matter how much easier it seems it would be if you did?

. . . .

When Will I Grow Up?

Sometimes I want to clean up my desk and go out and say, respect me, I'm a respectable grown-up, and other times I just want to jump into a paper bag and shake and bake myself to death.

—Wendy Wasserstein, *Uncommon Women and Others*

"School's out forever!" Alice Cooper screamed on the radio as I plopped my backpack into my mom's Buick on the last day of fifth grade. "I'm going to sing this song when I finish college," I announced confidently, having determined it would be an embarrassing rookie error to sing along until school really was a thing of the past. Yet despite my best attempts, I ended up being wrong anyway. Not just because I logged five more years of graduate school after college, but because as long as you're alive, no number of degrees gets you out for recess.

As Cooper (né Vincent Furnier in his early youth) describes in another one of his greatest hits, "I'm Eighteen": "Lines form on my face and hands . . . I'm a boy and

I'm a man." The title of this tune tells us that these are the musings of an eighteen-year-old, although I have to say this seems stressed-out for eighteen. Nonetheless, it captures how confoundingly nonlinear growing up can be. More often than not, despite having reached a specific age, milestone, or life-cycle ritual, we are young and old all at once.

How many times, long after eighteen, have you been shocked to realize that just when you think you know where you fit on the whole continuum of young and old, something knocks you off the grid? Like when you think of yourself as young, until someone calls you "sir" or "ma'am"? Or when a question posed to you—as it was to me recently by my ten-year-old sister, Eve—begins with the phrase, "In the olden days . . ." Maybe you've realized you've developed an inexplicable, yet instinctive, fear of teenagers traveling in packs. Or maybe you've assumed that "at *your* age" you should know more and have accomplished more, but that you have none of the comfort, status, or solidity you believed would be the natural result of all that time and effort.

Boy, man, woman, girl. We have to check one age range when filling out surveys, but we don't always feel like one checkmark is accurate enough. If we created more specific surveys for ourselves, we would have more boxes to check. For instance, a sixty-year-old man might feel like checking "18–25" in the category "What to Do with the Rest of My

Life (Since My Company Downsized and I Had to Take Early Retirement)." Similarly, the 101-year-old Queens, New York, woman who survived a pummeling by a mugger in his thirties might swagger toward "18–25" next to the "I Eat Punks Like You for Breakfast" box, despite the fact that she uses a walker to get around.

While I'll cop to having reached a point in my own life when I have begun to sing lyrics I once knew cold with far more incorrect phrases and awkward hums where the verses should be (which makes me feel like checking a box called "My Mother"), I am not so out of it yet that I'm unfamiliar with the online phenomenon that is *Wikipedia*. And whereas, in the olden days, I might have gone to *Webster's* for a definition of *adulthood*, I decided to see what I could find in Wikiville first. Given the democratic and anonymous nature of *Wikipedia*'s contributors, this entry actually could have been written by a precocious and computer-savvy ten-year-old. Regardless, the description rings true. It states, "There are some qualities that symbolize adultness in most cultures. Not always is there a concordance between the qualities and the physical age of the person." Bottom line: being an adult is not the same as growing up. One is a title conferred upon you at a certain age, in relationship to cultural or civic contexts, but it's an honorary one: show up, wear the robe, and—*boom*—you're a "Dr." It gets you a driver's license, a place in the military, a legal margarita, and discounted movie theater tickets. Growing up, however, is a constant state of becoming, and, oftentimes, an act of will.

This is particularly the case when a comfortable, familiar gait is far more attractive and less demanding than anything that might speed your heart rate. Consider Phoenix Suns basketball coach Mike D'Antoni's response in a 2007 *New York Times* interview to a comment made by his thirtysomething MVP point guard Steve Nash. Nash submitted that the Suns' run-'n'-gun style that averages the team more than one hundred points per game was entertaining to watch, but that it definitely took a nightly toll on the players. Coach D'Antoni had his own thoughts on the matter. "It might just take its toll worse if you walk and they beat the heck out of you," he said. "If you're playing a halfcourt set and you keep the floor not spaced, to me that's worse than not running. You run marathons when you're sixty years old; you can run." D'Antoni was not interested in excuses, not the least of which would be age.

Days of Birth

No one knows when people started putting candles on cakes to mark their birthdays and size up their lives by the numbers. The Asante in Ghana celebrate *krada*—a purification ritual practiced in large groups organized by the day of the week people were born, but without private, individual acknowledgments of actual birth dates. There is only one mention of a dedicated birthday celebration in the Torah: Pharoah's in the Book of Exodus. In America today, sidestepping individual birthdays could be an attractive trend, since, once a person passes the Chuck E. Cheese party and Jell-O-shot years, birthdays have become synonymous with hopping the express train to Botox and social invisibility. Somewhere along the line we started focusing intensely on aging as little more than a physical phenomenon with what a grade school teacher might call "negative attention." And it isn't just our society that does it. A few months before I turned thirty-five, I was treated to a Russian saying by my aesthetician, mid–bikini wax. "Until thirty-five, you are entering bazaar," she said, as I tried to go to my happy place. "After thirty-five," she continued, "you leaving it." I'm still not sure which part of that experience was more painful. But as Pete Townshend sings in "Split Skirts," "Can't pretend that growing older never hurts."

Even if we were to skip the whole birthday thing and see if it got us focused on growing up instead of getting older, we'd still have a variety of adulthood rituals that leave us stranded for guidance and meaning most of our lives. In Latino communities, a girl of fifteen steps into adulthood when she celebrates her *Quinceañera*, often-times switching from wearing flat shoes to heels to symbolize the transition. The 2006 film of the same name demonstrates how for some girls this rite of passage into adulthood is more about dresses and stretch Hummer limos than it is about growing up. For the main character, Magdalena, who becomes pregnant in the months leading up to her own *Quinceañera*, the circumstances of her life—not the life-cycle ceremony itself—move her into a whole new realm of grown-up decision making.

In the Jewish world, a girl becomes a bat mitzvah at the age of twelve and a boy becomes a bar mitzvah at the age of thirteen—literally "a son or daughter of obligation," one who assumes adult responsibility for religious choices. In ancient times, however, these transitions were not marked by public prayer gatherings or parties with awkward boy-girl dances to "Careless Whisper." Instead these milestones coincided with the onset of puberty and physical sexual maturity (replete with Talmudic descriptions that today's bat and bar mitzvah–aged kids would surely call "TMI—Too Much Information" about the number of, ahem, hairs one needs to attain adult communal status). In addition, early bar and bat mitzvah details included a blessing for parents to utter, relieving them of any responsibility for the things their children—having officially entered adulthood—might do. Apparently helicopter parenting was not on the rabbinic radar screen in those days. Nor was the fact that the "today I am a man" phenomenon commonly associated with bar mitzvah is really just the beginning of growing into manhood. As a matter of fact, more and more frequently men and women from twenty-two to seventy are deciding to become bar and bat mitzvah (as a close friend of mine did to mark her fortieth birthday), making the conscious decision to publicly affirm their grown-up status in, and responsibility for, the community on a timeline they've created.

While these ceremonies have the potential to be meaningful at any age, there is far more growing up over the course of a lifetime than there are ritualized rites of passage to mark them. Some fourteen Hindu rites of passage, called *samskaras*, exist from conception to marriage, including celebrating first haircuts and the beginning of study. The only *samskara* after the wedding, however, is death. It is not much different outside of religious frameworks, in which we equate reaching certain milestones, like graduation, landing a dream job, getting married, and becoming a parent with growing up. Yet the scripted moments that constitute growing up often proclaim a profound personal evolution prematurely, directly or indirectly encouraging us to crumple up our developmental to-do lists and toss them in the trash.

At a party, my friends Amanda and Meir, both of whom are highly accomplished working professionals and wonderful parents, and I chatted with their four-year-old son. He made excellent conversation, but he also made it quite clear when he was ready to go home, which was about twenty minutes before Mommy and Daddy were. Protracted adult good-byes at dinner parties can be hard enough on the adults, let alone on a little one who has done a yeoman's job of discussing the finer points of SpongeBob, Batman, and Spiderman, and has correctly identified and done impressions of all the animals on Ole McDonald's farm. As Amanda carefully and responsibly got her son buckled for a safe roll home in the stroller she looked up and said, "We're his mom and dad, but we're still kids, too."

The growing-up landmarks we know do not exhaust the ones we might have. You can be parents and "When Will I Grow Up?" can be your question. You can get *AARP Magazine* and it can be your question. You can be married, divorced, trying to have a child, an adult child of a parent whose loss you're mourning, a grandparent, financially set, respected in your chosen field, and, still, this could be your question.

While valuable experience and wisdom do automatically accrue with age, a desire for some finality in growth can make our lives smaller than they're meant to be. If we hear "When Will I Grow Up?" as "When will I *ever* grow up?" it's as if somehow we've received a demotion. If, however, we can experience the question as the gateway to an unexpected, unscripted rite of passage that will expand our lives, the answers we find will give us more moments—not fewer—to anticipate and ultimately celebrate. In fact, keeping the question alive may breathe new life into where we've chosen to be now, making us more effective, creative, and engaged doing exactly what we've been doing. If we train ourselves to stop waiting for the one moment when the question will be answered, and rather find a variety of answers inside ourselves in many moments, we will never settle for being anything less than we can be.

That is why asking when you'll grow up doesn't mean abandoning your commitments, nor does it mean wandering aimlessly from whim to whim, or throwing your hands up in the air as if you have no control over or responsibility for your actions. On the contrary, if you understand this question as an opening to perpetually, consciously choosing what you do with your time in life, you will feel less adrift. That may mean finding the inspiration to deepen or transform existing obligations, or uncovering the strength to pursue new paths that reveal aspects of self you never would have known existed.

Always growing up can make a "yes" you've already uttered even more emphatic and a "no" definitive enough to free you for other things.

To Lives!

Some say life would be easier if we had fewer choices. Over Indian food one night, my friend Gabrielle, a thirty-three-year-old professionally trained soprano and part owner of a successful Manhattan business, wondered whether we're meant to have so many choices to begin with. She talked about her parents, how they didn't puzzle over their lives, their careers, or their purpose in the same way that she and her friends do. For instance, she pointed out, her father had two choices when it came to his profession: doctor or lawyer. He couldn't stand the sight of blood, so he went to law school. Gabrielle's mother taught school until she got married, at which point her job became being a wife and mother. "Maybe we shouldn't have all these options," Gabrielle said. I suggested that, in fact, the opposite is true, that human beings are built for options. That, in the words of the band Switchfoot, "We were meant to live for so much more." I said to Gabrielle that it's when we pretend we have no choices and that we're all grown up in a definitive checklist fashion, that we lose ourselves and our chances to be the most we've been created to be.

Imagine a world in which Mahatma Gandhi, who married at the age of thirteen, had never left India to study law in England. Then imagine if he'd remained content with his choice to be a lawyer, if he'd spent the rest of his days having decided he was all grown up, with nothing new to do, and nothing more to offer. Where would every woman whose vote is counted each election day be if, as a young girl, Susan B. Anthony had accepted her teacher's declaration that a girl "[only] needs to know how to read her Bible and count her egg money, nothing more"? What if, with that, she had decided that once she had acquired those skills she would have arrived at the finish line of womanhood? Try to see a world where the color of an athlete's skin keeps him from playing in a world-class athletic event, even though he's the world's number one player. If you can't, thank Arthur Ashe for seeing that he had far more to grow beyond winning championships when he got the apartheid-riddled South African Open eliminated from the tennis tour. These are people who knew they had many lives to live over the course of their one lifetime. They have changed our lives because of it.

Being made for a lifetime of growing up doesn't only

apply to those whose names appear in history books or whose words are quoted in speeches. The business my friend Gabrielle co-owns is a family affair. She and her brother, father, and mother, all from Ohio, took a chance on the food industry (a commercial arena with one of the highest failure rates anywhere) by opening a small chain of coffee shops in New York City. On any given day you can find Gabrielle, her brother, Jonathan, and her parents, Alice and Richard, working in their beautiful, award-winning coffeehouses that have been lauded in the press. The reason their shops are so special has nothing to do with the media attention or accolades, but with the unique way their combined talents have created oases of real communal connection on an island of millions where it's easy to be a stranger. None of this could have come into being if Richard hadn't imagined another life beyond retirement from his thriving law practice, or if Jonathan hadn't given up his career representing actors to become a passionate expert on roasting, brewing, and serving the perfect cup of coffee. It couldn't have happened if Alice hadn't expanded her skills as a mother, and her background as a dancer, to make customers feel like they've got a hip, caring mom serving them their morning muffins. And if Gabrielle hadn't decided to step off the opera tour merry-go-round to make the coffeehouse her stage, she might not have discovered her talent for triathlons or started a running club that is a neighborhood phenomenon. We all have a next rite of passage if we choose it.

It's not uncommon to hear the phrase "You only live once." While we may have varying beliefs about what happens to us after we die, we are all united in our mortality. As the Koran teaches:

> We cause to remain in the womb whatever We please for an appointed term, and then We bring you forth as infants that you may grow up and reach your prime. Some die young, and some live on to abject old age when all that they once knew they know no more.

As discussed in many ancient traditions like this one, and as evidenced by the power of how quickly someone can be with us in one moment and gone the next, we learn that we come into the world by forces beyond ourselves, and we similarly leave the world without a scheduled appointment on our day planner. However, what happens in between the days of our births and the moments when we draw our last breaths is another matter entirely. On the HBO series *Six Feet Under*, a grieving woman asks Nate, the funeral home director played by Peter Krause (no relation), why people have to die. He replies, "To keep life precious."

We are always growing, until we are not. So while we may only live once, we don't have to wait to die in order to have multiple incarnations. The Hebrew word *chaim*, meaning "life," is actually plural; when translated it literally means "lives." If you've ever heard the popular toast, *"L'chaim!"*—"To life!"—you are actually hearing people say, "To lives!" Just as we are built with the ability to use fear to break through to new beginnings, we are also born with the capacity to live many different lives over the course of one lifetime. In *The Sound of Music*, Sister Maria zings the yet-to-be-smitten Captain von Trapp with a keen observation: "Activity suggests a life filled with purpose." With this she comments on her dour employer's full schedule and highly regimented existence—all the hallmarks of a real adult. But she's more than subtly implying that being busy and growing are not necessarily the same thing. We can easily do one perfectly respectable thing for a long time—forever even—without stopping to examine whether it's all we're here to do or be.

Ignoring the ever-present imperative to choose your lives by constantly growing into them is the most unsafe move you can make, and not just because you may find yourself feeling unhappy or discontented. It's bigger than that. Relinquishing that choice not only affects your personal outlook and productivity, it keeps you from maximizing what you uniquely have to offer others—

personally, communally, even globally. If you limit your life by eliminating the choices that come with truly living, you'll never know what you're keeping yourself from and the lives you could change, even in the tiniest ways.

When a person's age is given in the Bible, the years are broken down into sections. Take the matriarch Sarah, who is said to have been 127 years old at the time of her death. In Genesis, the Hebrew text says, literally, "Sarah was one hundred years and seven years and twenty years. These are the *lives* of Sarah." These are Sarah's *lives*. Perhaps now, more than ever, this description can help us see that we can bundle multiple life segments into a lifetime, during which we expect to serve different purposes at different points. As such, instead of being paralyzed by a lifetime of choices, either by hiding from choice or becoming so overwhelmed we choose nothing at all, we can see these different bundles of time as opportunities for different lives. We can see outgrowing an identity, a job, or a goal as a natural part of being alive; we can see that choosing a new chapter doesn't mean that the things we move on from weren't real, just that it was time to be more. As my friend Shelley says, "Becoming something new doesn't mean losing yourself. You just add a layer."

Adding layers keeps the days precious.

If something is making you feel like a kid again, in the sense that you feel an acute lack of control over your life's path, "When Will I Grow Up?" is your question. If you cannot avoid, perhaps for the first time, the feeling (or fact) that you have no idea what's coming next, this is your question. If you sense you can go on living precisely the same way, but that if you do you won't be able to live with yourself, this is your question.

What Would My Mother Think?

When I spoke with my friend Daniel about this chapter, he immediately said, "You mean, like, what would my mother think?" He instantly equated the notion of growing up with seeing his choices in relationship to those of his parents, either resulting in their approval or disapproval. I've heard people utter this phrase before, and the curious thing is that often they are mothers and fathers who lost their own parents long ago. No matter how old we get, an instinct reminds us that we will forever be someone's child. We always hear our parents' voices along with our own. Apparently this is a natural mammalian trait. I recall learning that when a baby dolphin is first born, its mother will whistle to it nonstop. She does this to imprint her sound on the baby, so the baby will recognize her. But the baby also has to develop its own signature whistle, which, in the dolphin world, is the equivalent of having a name. So without a distinctive whistle, one dolphin is the same as the next.

So how do humans develop their signature whistles? A sixteenth-century commentary on a passage from the Book of Genesis offers one perspective. If you missed earlier episodes of adventures in Genesis and are joining the show already in progress, here's the back story: We meet Abraham, one of the Bible's leading men, when he gets the equivalent of a critical *Mission: Impossible*–style recorded message—except this one is "live" and comes from God. Abraham's mission, should he choose to accept it, is to "go forth from your native land, from the place of your birth, from your father's house, to the land I will show you." Much has been made throughout the centuries about the great detail used to basically say, "Leave here and go there." A Hasidic teaching handed down from generation to generation illuminates the seeming verbosity:

> God says to the human being: First you must leave your native land, meaning who the world says you are. Then your birthplace, meaning whom your mother says you are. Then your father's house, meaning whom your father says you are. Only then will you be able to go to the land I will show you.

Abraham does light out on the expedition, without so much as a picture postcard of the destination or a visit to the land's official website. He is seventy-five years old at the time. At an advanced age, Abraham only first realizes he has a wild card.

We all have wild cards—aspects of who we are that cannot be connected to either parent in any way, expressions that are entirely unique to our lives. The wild card is my interpretation of an ancient Jewish belief that three partners participate in the creation of a human being: the Holy One (God), a father, and a mother. In this context, I have always seen the Holy One as that wild card—the unknown that resides in every person and has nothing to do with nature or nurture, but with something bigger: a surprise that unfolds through our lives.

When we first meet Abraham, he is in a phase of life people rarely associate with growth. Yet he exemplifies what it means to grow up when you're "grown," to refuse to be propelled forward by the sheer momentum of what has already been set in motion—whether by a mother's expectations, a father's approbation, or how the world has come to know you. Perhaps you've moved along a certain course, even one that you like, without ever having said, "This is the direction I want to take." You've worked hard and strategized to get where you are, yet instead of feeling at home at a point it may have taken you decades to reach, you have the sense you've wandered into a strange land almost as if by accident. You realize that you've said "I will because I can" or "I will because I always have," but you've never said, "I will because I must." You realize you have choices, but the choices involve multiple positives and not one obvious negative. These are all opportunities to grow up because they let you show more of your wild card.

Our parents are our first teachers, and, regardless of whether our relationships with them were or are positive, conflicted, or both, they make the biggest impression on us, even in their absence (often to many peoples' great shock). But if you're an adult who cannot hear the call of "When Will I Grow Up?" over the din of "What would my mother (or father) think?", you'll deny yourself, your loved ones (including your parents or your parents' memory), your children (present or future), work colleagues, and the world the full offerings of your destiny. And your parents will not be to blame for imposing those limits. The blame will rest with you.

Playing Your Wild Card

Two women with the same name offer different examples of the wild card factor. Not long ago, pop queen Madonna adopted the moniker of another queen, by the name of Esther, through her study of Kabbalah. For a woman so successfully and consistently committed to changing her identity over time, Madonna could not have chosen a better spiritual pseudonym. If the story of the biblical Queen Esther's life isn't quite as familiar to you as Madonna's, I'll refresh your memory, because the original Esther's experience deserves a listen.

Back in the day—the day being fifth-century Persia—a king named Ahasuerus was looking for a new wife. In the absence of Match.com and *The Bachelor*, Ahasuerus had to find a mate the old-fashioned way: by holding a giant beauty pageant. Esther, known for her exquisite features and charm, aces out thousands of others in this ancient version of *America's Next Top Model*. Frankly, it's not much of a contest; as the story goes, the minute King Ahasuerus catches a glimpse of Esther, he's a goner.

Being queen agrees with Esther. It plays to the strengths she's known her whole life—or, more specifically, to one of them: being hot. But she's hiding something behind the glamour: neither the king nor anyone in his court knows that Esther is Jewish.

Yet this part of her identity is not the most important thing about Esther that remains concealed. In the Talmud, we learn that the name *Esther* derives from the Hebrew word meaning "to hide." But the Bible itself tells us that Esther has another name, too: Hadassah, or "myrtle," in English. In the biblical psalms, myrtles are associated with righteousness and righteous people. So while these days a kid named Myrtle has a good chance of dining solo in the school cafeteria, in Queen Esther's story, her second name suggests that there are aspects of her personality that even she is not aware of waiting to be revealed. That hidden name tips the wild card in her hand.

Meanwhile, Haman, the royal court equivalent to a schoolyard bully, is crafting a plot to murder all of Persia's Jews. When Esther's uncle Mordecai—her adoptive father from a young age following her parents' death—catches wind of the plan, he sends her a message imploring her to burst into the king's chambers, spill the beans about her Jewish roots, and bring Haman's nasty plan to a grinding halt. Esther's reply is simple: anyone who enters the king's inner court without being summoned is killed. Since she has not been summoned, she won't be going.

Mordecai refuses to take no for an answer and sends another note to his reluctant niece. This time his message contains a question that not only has the potential to significantly alter the life of Esther's people, but also to change Esther's life forever. Mordecai asks, "Did you ever think maybe you were created for precisely this moment?" Mordecai's question moves Esther to grow up and play her wild card, withholding nothing of her life's unique unfolding from herself or from the people who are counting on her the most. She talks to the king, and, as a result, Esther foils Haman's bloody scheme. Rejoicing ensues in the land (along with a few beheadings).

In the movie version of this story, the credits would roll. But in life off the screen, the cameras keep rolling, and we're off to the next challenge, the next rite of passage.

Madonna easily could have let the credits roll on her life long ago, too, if she'd wanted. Yet she's still asking "When Will I Grow Up?"—still finding and playing her wild card. From "Material Girl" to "Ray of Light," from single to married to motherhood and adoption, Madonna shows us that there's always more hidden inside waiting to come out. No wonder she wants us to call her Esther.

We know that any questions that exist to help us grow can be exciting and liberating, but at the same time we tend to avoid them because we know from experience that mirth and personal momentum don't always go hand-in-hand. However, if we, like both Esthers, keep ourselves from turning our backs on the surprise rites of passage to be, we might avoid the pain of regret that usually comes when there isn't time left on the clock for more chances. So don't wait for your uncle Mordecai to prod, or for Mom or Dad to praise. Push yourself to keep growing as long as you have breath, and you'll bridge the distance between living your potential and imagining (or avoiding) it. While you may fall into your growing-up moments serendipitously, more often than not if you really want to play your wild card you'll have to decide to play it.

Part of finding your answer to "When Will I Grow Up?" is, as my teacher Rabbi Yitz Greeenberg says, "betting on yourself."

You must, of course, take into account the people in your life who are affected by how you place your bets. This includes getting clear about why this is a wild card moment and how badly you need it to grow the life you want to lead. As college basketball coach Billy Gillispie, known for his eccentricities and what some would call crazy devotion to the sport, said in a *New York Times* interview in the thick of 2007 March Madness, "What my being requires for happiness is totally different. I understand, I'm a different person." To be able to say that, and say it with confidence, is growing up.

Heroes

In Cameron Crowe's film *Elizabethtown*, the protagonist, Drew, considered to be somewhat of a prodigy, devotes eight years of his life to creating a gym shoe—a shoe that turns out to be flawed and costs his company nearly a billion dollars in losses. In a blink, he loses his job, his girlfriend, and his entire sense of what he's here to do. As he describes it: "No true fiasco ever began as a quest for mere adequacy. A motto of the British Special Service Air Force is, 'Those who risk, win.' A single green vine shoot is able to grow through cement. The Pacific Northwestern salmon beats itself bloody on its quest to travel hundreds of miles upstream, against the current, with a single purpose: sex, of course. But also life."

We've all experienced our own version of Drew's story, a time when we've risked big and lost bigger. A time when we've felt certain we've reached our "all grown-up" moment of moments, only to experience disappointment and failure, have our resolve, our sense of self, and our sense of humor tested. This shared experience fills Joseph Campbell's statement from his epic work *The Hero with a Thousand Faces* with truth: "The hero is the champion of things becoming, not of things become." In our walk through life, in our drive to reach The Moment, it's easy to forget that the walk itself, rather than the arrival at the destination, is the only guarantee. In the meantime, we can all be heroes as long as we maintain our commitment to becoming.

In my living room hangs a framed copy of Alberto

Giacometti's *Walking Man II*. Giacometti eventually turned the sketch into a life-size bronze statue, but this drawing I look at every day holds its own fascination. It's basically a stick figure in profile—tiny head, barely any indication of arms, and uncooked spaghetti strands for legs. Yet even though the figure is spindly and slight, his bionic motion makes the sketch a wonder. The man's long legs take up most of his body; he's captured midstride, with a giant back foot, heel facing skyward, pushing his front foot forward. You get the sense that, no matter what, he'll keep on walking.

I brought my Giacometti drawing home from a London museum shop because home is the place we go at the end of long days when the world may leave us feeling deflated, like we're little more than stick figures. When I see *Walking Man*, I'm reminded there's more ahead, that my story, that the human story—even in the face of failure and fiasco—goes on. It's one way I've found to remind myself that I'm always growing up, to ask myself when I will. Regardless of what inspires the question in you, it's the asking that sparks a desire to find your answer. And as long as you're alive, an answer is always waiting; nothing—not royal position, stardom, a good job, a nice home, a great relationship, or a particular birthday—keeps any of us from being forever on the way to something more.

So as you begin to use "When Will I Grow Up?" to its fullest potential in your life, be honest with yourself: when you know you're using your age to pass off reticence as maturity, remind yourself it's time to grow up. When you try to pass off world-wariness as wisdom, thumb through the deck for your wild card. You'll need to challenge yourself to use your life experience to grow again, rather than using it as an excuse for relinquishing your exuberance for living.

A Quiet Thing

You should also expect that the growing up we do when we're older, particularly the growing up we take on voluntarily, usually happens quietly. In the words of the 1960s Broadway songwriting team of Kander and Ebb, "Happiness comes in on tiptoe ... It's a quiet thing." Your next growing-up moment may not come with the applause that accompanies candles going out with one breath, being lifted on a chair with people dancing in circles around you, or with any witnesses other than you. But how it brings out your wild card shapes you and affects how you share your new growth through your actions with others, will be its own celebration.

One night, a friend of mine and I were out to dinner.

The restaurant manager, with whom we'd talked on occasion, came over to say hello. My friend noticed a thin silver chain around his neck and she, being far more outgoing than I, reached out to examine it. It turned out that the chain held a coin that he had gotten "when he became a man." At first even my highly extroverted dining companion didn't know how to respond. Because we didn't know him well, we weren't sure if he meant it was a memento associated with a cultural or religious ceremony, something he got when he lost his virginity, or a gift from his doctor following gender reassignment surgery. Seeing that we were both confused and reluctant to inquire further, he volunteered his story.

He was in his twenties and traveling in Greece with friends. While he was there, he spotted a monastery perched high on a mountaintop that was neither marked nor made for climbing. Yet having seen it, "When Will I Grow Up?" became his question. He decided that he needed to scale that mountain alone and create his own rite of passage into manhood. And so he did. Along the way, he had to let his water plummet to the ground to hang on and avoid what could have been a fatal fall when the climb got far more difficult than he had expected. As the water fell, it soaked his socks through and through, resulting in bloody blistering and chafing on his feet and ankles as he continued this quest of his design. He did make it to the top, but he had to get back down before nightfall, so as not to alarm his friends.

In the end, he made it all the way down in tremendous pain, but alive. However, his friends were not waiting to welcome the mythic hero back from his adventures. Instead, he was met by a raging forest fire. So instead of walking a straight line through that area toward the village where they all were staying, he had to go a much greater distance around the fire to avoid being consumed by it. As we listened to this tale, I remember him saying, "At that point I must have sat down at least three times on the way, just wanting to die."

Obviously he got back up enough times to save, and claim, his life. Grateful to be in one piece, he went out by himself the next day and bought what to anyone else, including him under different conditions, would have been, as he called it, "a cheesy tourist's souvenir." It was a flimsy replica of an ancient coin engraved with hieroglyphics. To him, though, it marked a moment when he grew up.

Whether you're scaling an actual mountain or just sense that you're way out on a limb, "When Will I Grow Up?" is guiding you to an unwritten rite of passage of your own. You won't need a pair of hiking boots, but you will need to begin to find your answer by determining what's sending the question into your world. Whatever it is, the question needn't signify failure or lack of achievement; it is a sign of life. It's an indication that life is offering you a chance to go to school again, but without the pencils, books, or the teachers' dirty looks.

You can't go back to childhood (and would you go back to seventh grade again, even if someone paid you?), but you can always grow up. You can be an accomplished, conscientious, confident adult, but as long as you're alive, some part of your existence will always say, "Time to grow up. Again."

Y O U R   H I G H L I G H T E R

Now it's your turn to use your highlighter. Everybody's got one, and it will help you discover your answer to this question. It could be an instinct to linger a little longer in a conversation you wouldn't otherwise have found interesting, being drawn to an activity you'd forgotten you enjoyed or never imagined you'd want to pursue, or it might be the discovery of a dream deferred that suddenly seems to be beckoning to you from every corner of your world. Whatever form it takes, let your highlighter lead you to what you don't realize you already know, or to that something you're trying to know for yourself, by yourself, today.

- What is making you feel more acutely that you have no idea what's coming next?

- What aspect of your wild card could be connected to that feeling?

- What do you need to do to develop more of your wild card?

- What stands between you and your current rite of passage?

- In order for this rite of passage to occur, do you need to push or do you need to be patient?

- Is there a moment right now that you sense is calling you to "add a new layer?" What kind of growing would you need to do, even if you aren't yet certain you can, in order to rise to the occasion?

Who's Got My Back?

You were turning me around to look at myself. For I had placed myself behind my own back, refusing to see myself.

—Saint Augustine, *Confessions of a Sinner*

Over the course of our lives we inherit and develop a variety of ties with others. Some are enduring, some are situational, yet all hold meaning and truth. In reflecting on friendships, for instance, Ralph Waldo Emerson writes, "When they are real, they are not glass threads or frostwork, but the solidest thing we know." The Bible teaches that we should love our neighbors as ourselves, and that we should take care of the strangers in our midst. And, of course, we learn at any early age that we are to honor our parents.

In fact, much of what we spend time learning and unlearning about relationships begins with our families.

Long before the term *dysfunction* was included in discussions of family ties, fathers, mothers, brothers, and sisters were riding along, *Little Miss Sunshine*–style, in unreliable recreational vehicles filled with jealousy, respect, resentment, pride, joy, and the occasional murder. When it comes to family, the stuff of Greek mythology, Shakespeare, and the Bible may not exactly imitate our own lives (and thank goodness for that!), but it does help tell the story of who we are in our lifetimes: who we aspire to be and who we try our very best to avoid becoming.

I've often heard people talk about the families we choose, as opposed to the families into which we are born. It's an oft-repeated phrase because it's true. We do not choose our families, but even when we have the most wonderful friends and have a partner and children of our own, our parents and siblings carry information that we will always need, even if the relationships aren't the ones we want or ones we maintain. For instance, biblical Isaac never, ever speaks another word to his father, Abraham, after Abraham comes close to sacrificing him out of fealty to God (and who can blame him?), but Isaac is there to lay Abraham to rest. And, not only is Isaac present at the burial of Abraham, but so is Isaac's older brother, Ishmael—someone to whom he's gone practically his entire life without speaking. The two men are strangers, and yet they share a unique bond: they are sons of the same father, brothers, no matter whom they "adopt" as their chosen parents or their chosen siblings. The Bible makes a point of noting, as well, that Jacob and Esau tend to the burial of their father, Isaac, together, even though they have served as definite prototypes for extreme sibling alienation, battling each other for their father's blessing and affection. And Jacob's children, the favored son, Joseph, and his jealous brothers, reunited to carry their father's bones out of Egypt, even after suffering one of the worst sibling rifts on record. They go decades without seeing each other after the boys go right up to the line of murdering the spoiled Daddy's boy, opting to hand Joseph over as strangers' chattel instead. It's something straight out of a bizarre Court TV case.

My mom has always quoted a teaching from Lebanese poet Kahlil Gibran's "The Prophet": "Your children are not your children. . . . They come through you but not from you, and though they are with you, yet they belong not to you." This may be the case, but whether our siblings get us or we never get them, they *are* our siblings. And our parents *are* our parents. Even if we make a conscious point, whether for our sanity or for our safety, to steer clear of them in real time, it doesn't mean we don't, or won't, have to face those relationships in order to face ourselves fully some day.

I have three younger siblings—two sisters and a

brother aged thirty-two, ten, and seven, respectively. The age differential has to do with the fact that I have three parents—my mother, my father, and my stepmother, who has been in my life since my adolescence. And now I'm going to do something that could get me in trouble with all of them (even though I'm an adult and technically can't be in trouble with my parents anymore): I'm going to air (imagine these next two words uttered in a hushed tone) "family business."

My father and his sister do not speak, and neither do my mother and her sister—they did not for many years of my childhood, and they continue to exist without even the slightest acknowledgment of one another to this day. Yet one of my most distinct memories is from my paternal grandmother's funeral. Jewish funerals are not conducted with open caskets, but if the family requests, they can spend some time with the deceased prior to the memorial service and burial. At the age of fourteen, I watched from the way back of the funeral home chapel through a half-open door, as my father and his sister stood before their mother's casket. At first I thought they were crying, which they were, but then I noticed that they were laughing, too. Something about what they imagined she would have thought or said in that moment that only they, as her children, could know had sent them giggling at a less than appropriate time. Something only they could know. I've seen it happen with my mother and her sister, too—in happy times and in sad ones. A window opens and they are children together again: the only ones who share a certain part of each other's history from an exclusive vantage point. I see this same phenomenon when I officiate at funerals, as well. Even when people aren't talking to one another, and have made a point of saying they do not when we meet prior to the service, their hands are suddenly clasped when the moment of saying good-bye arrives. It doesn't mean their relationship to one another changes. But a part of it reappears when their lives are changing as they communicate their grief in a way that can be understood by no one else.

I experienced this phenomenon for myself, although fortunately not in a funeral setting. Several years ago, my mother had to go in for emergency surgery, which included the possibility of the doctors finding cancer. Even with the love and support of my grandma (her mother), long-time friends, and a whole community, I have never felt closer to my sister Stephanie than during the hours waiting for the procedure to be done; spending time with Mom during her hospital stay and making certain she was receiving the proper care, medications, and attention; and then helping with her recovery at home (not that she would let us help very much!). No one else knew our mom like we did, and no one else ever would.

No one else would feel precisely the same gratitude we did, and still do, that she is her usual healthy, vibrant self. That is a profound truth—whether we talk on the phone once a week or once every six months, whether we have shared interests or very few.

The same goes for parents. Whether they've been absent or present, active or aloof, selfless or selfish, there is that honor thing. Long before Freud and Jung, the ancient rabbis understood the complex relationship between parents and children. They did not countenance abuse and drew limits on how much any child should have to endure at a parent's misguided hands. They were harsh, as well, on parents who failed to teach their children important life skills, including things as basic as learning how to swim. But they also taught that whatever parents did not teach us as children—and our parents, no matter how wonderful or well-intentioned cannot teach us everything—we have to learn ourselves. Overall, though, the ancients found the obligation to honor one's parents so complex that they defined the parameters of the law in surprisingly basic terms. They held that an adult child should make certain a parent had food and shelter, but left the rest open for interpretation based on individual circumstances.

It is to this that I add two additional elements that will help us further explore the question, your question,

"Who's Got My Back?" The first I attribute to my friend and colleague Roderick, whose interpretation of what it means to honor one's father and mother has become a part of my own teaching and my own life. Sometimes the best that we can do is bring honor to our parents through who we are and who we become. This is something we can choose, and it has little to do with whether or not we believe our parents are due honor for their parenting, if they left us early in life, or if we've ever had a chance to know them at all.

Singer Billy Joel's father left the scene very early in the piano man's life. For all intents and purposes, they were strangers. A 2003 article in a New York neighborhood paper called the *Villager* captures Joel's memory of the visit. "It was . . . strained," Joel said. "No animosity. But I was puzzled. Why hadn't I heard from him in all those years? But then I realized he'd had plenty of trouble in his life, beginning with the Nazis . . . the people lost at Auschwitz . . . an unsuccessful marriage in America." After many years, in 2001, Joel recorded a classical album, *Fantasies & Delusions*, at the Mozartsaal Koncerthaus in Vienna, where his father still lives, and his brother, Alex, is a well-known conductor. Joel saw his father as a man, and that vision shaped his own vision of himself. By his account, it reopened him to a love of classical music he had set aside for a substantial and rewarding period of time in his life, but that beckoned for his return of focus. However strained their relationship had been or may continue to be, they managed to get each other's backs in profound ways.

Which brings me to the second teaching significant to the question; this one from an Italian film, Marco Tullio Giordana's *The Best of Youth* (2003) chronicling one family's experiences over forty years, from 1966 to 2000, through sweeping political and personal changes. One of the storylines is that of a mother who abandons her young daughter for her passionate commitment to the Red Brigades. Later forced to go underground for crimes against the government, she misses her daughter Sara's entire young life and early adulthood. On the eve of Sara's wedding, she reveals to her father, Nicola (who has raised her single-handedly), that her mother has written her a letter saying that she is alive and well in Florence and trying to start her life over again. This is the dialogue that ensues:

Sara: What should I do?
Nicola: Depends on how strong you feel. Are you
   happy?
Sara: Of course!
Nicola: Well, then now is the time to be generous.

We call these relationships the ties that bind, not always because we feel close, but because they are part of the connective tissue of who we are. For instance, what of Sara's joy could be diminished by unburdening herself—even if temporarily—of her own feelings of anger and bewilderment, of having been grossly shortchanged by her mother's actions or inaction? Even when people don't "have your back," in the sense of protecting you, they do own a piece of you, a piece that can show you more of who you are, that can help you be the person you want to be in your life.

We tend to think of the phrase *got my back* in terms of someone protecting us, but really, as adults we are our own protectors, first and foremost. Therefore, these important relationships, which may run the gamut from fraught to fruitful and everything in between, all show us something in ourselves that we cannot see without their help—like trying to get a good look at your own back when you're dressing alone at home. No one can get a 360-degree view, even with the best mirror, solo.

So, for starters, finding your answer to "Who's Got My Back?" does not only have to do with who's looking out for you, but with who brings out more in you—for better and for worse.

Tugs and Kisses

In one of her diary entries Anaïs Nin once observed, "Each friend represents a world in us, a world possibly not born until they arrive, and it is only by this meeting that a new world is born." The Sufi mystic Rumi's first encounter with his good friend Shams of Tabriz, recounted in Barks's *The Soul of Rumi*, is a beautiful example of Nin's teaching. Just when Rumi thinks he knows himself, the world, and what he is meant to do in it, a new world opens for him in the form of an unexpected friendship. Standing at the banks of a river, teaching from his father's writings, Rumi is stunned when Shams pushes all of his books into the water. Naturally Rumi asks Shams who he is and what he thinks he's doing. Shams replies, "You must now live what you've been reading about." Seeing Rumi's pained expression at the sight of the wet books taking on more and more water, Shams thinks better of his actions, saying, "We can retrieve them. They'll be as dry as they were to start." Yet Rumi takes a look at his new friend and says, "Leave them. What I had thought of before as God I met today in a human being."

My father has always said that if you can count your true friends on one hand you should consider yourself lucky. But what makes a true friend? How do we discern between connections that are meant to create worlds for a moment and those that create universes that endure for a lifetime? How do we maintain those relationships, prioritize when so much else in life threatens to diminish them, particularly in a time when we are pulled in so many different directions? As the Rolling Stones remark in "Waiting on a Friend," we need people in our lives to cry to and we need people to protect. This is another aspect to "having your back," which figures prominently into making and maintaining friendships. Knowing who has your back doesn't only mean determining who'll be there for you, but understanding who needs you to be there—that what you have to offer is essential to the life of that friend. This combination is a key form of reciprocity, but one not to be confused with keeping score.

Keeping score leaves winners and losers, which applies on the court, out on the field, or in the boardroom. But in friendships, if you're the kind of friend you are because you're expecting someone else to be that exact same kind of friend in return, or because you're trying to "out-friend" another, you'll often be disappointed, and feel empty or angry. In those moments, you have to ask yourself if your reaction is because that person really isn't there for you, or if it's because you're waiting for quid pro quo responses that mirror precisely the way you like to be there for others. If you're keeping score, no one can have your back because you'll find countless reasons to get your back up, and you certainly won't be able to allow yourself to be open to new worlds by the other person. You're trying to control the world of your friendship, which can leave both parties feeling exiled. Be the kind of friend that is an extension of who you are and what you believe is your standard for having someone's back, but not as an example of the way someone should be a friend to you. And if a friendship you care about is falling short in some way, or if your friend tells you the same, see it as an opportunity for another aspect of your friendship to come into being. Conflict does not always signal the end of a friendship, but may in fact be the start of a much more significant connection.

I remember sitting on my friend David's roof deck one summer's evening. We were talking and ended up butting heads over something I can't even remember now. When the smoke cleared, and we had drunk some champagne, David raised his glass in a toast, saying, "Now that we have had a real disagreement, we are true friends." We had, in fact, known each other at that point for several years already. I thought we were already "true friends," and David's toast seemed particularly odd since I thought the goal of friendship was to get along—you know, play nicely. Yet, as I thought more about it, we didn't really know each other until there was something at stake, until we knew what made the other hurt or get angry just as well as we knew what made the other laugh. I found David's lesson to me later reflected in an ancient hieroglyphic manuscript recommended to me by my friend Chris (I read it in translation; Chris can read it in the original). The manuscript is called "The Instruction of Ptah-Hotep," a collection of life lessons written by an Egyptian governor as a legacy to his son. On the subject of friendship, it reads:

> If thou wouldest seek out the nature of a friend, ask it not of any companion of his; but pass a time with him alone, that thou injure not his affairs. Debate with him after a season: test his heart in an occasion of speech. When he hath told thee his past life, he hath made an opportunity that thou may either be ashamed for him or be familiar with him. Be not reserved with him when he openeth speech, neither answer after a scornful matter. Withdraw not thyself from him. . . .

Different connections inspire different worlds. You cannot know who might have your back based on someone else's opinion of that person, nor without some testing of the relationship, taking risks, revealing what you really think, sharing experiences you've had. Often the most unlikely pairings in friendship teach us the most about who we are—something so much harder to come by as we get older and begin to think we have passed the time in life when new friends can be made, as our circles of relationship close ranks. In any case, whether it's a new friend, an old one, or a connection lost and rediscovered, someone who's got your back, to paraphrase Train's lyrics to "Drops of Jupiter," will always stick up for you, "even when I know you're wrong." At the same time, those friends will tell you what they really think in private, choosing their moments carefully, letting you decide whether to take the advice or criticism or lay it aside, without ever laying you aside as a friend. They will cheer for you, even when they would rather curl up in silence with their own struggles, and you will be excited for them even if you are struggling with a down cycle in your own life. Someone who has your back will argue with you without abandoning you because they want you to be you, rather than making themselves more comfortable by requiring that you be more like them.

Rare are the friends who can stand to see you struggle, who remain with you throughout the many roads you'll take in life—including the ones they might see as detours or dead ends. One of the hardest things to experience is when a friend can't or won't ride with you anymore, when a fork in the road means a permanent parting of ways. This usually has less to do with you than with the other person. If something a friend sees in your life causes him or her too much pain, it often has to do with pain he already owns, rather than something you caused by living your life the way you deem necessary. Nonetheless, the separation is no less painful, no less of a loss. Anyone you have traveled even a little bit of the way with is enough a part of you—and you them—for it to hurt. In this regard, a person who has your back doesn't only prop you up, but pushes you forward, even if he or she is not someone who can or will travel forward in life by your side.

As important as it is to sustain and fight for the friendships we hold dear, knowing how to see when a world you've created through your friendship is signaling a good-bye is just as crucial as it was when you and that person chose to move beyond superficial hellos. It is in this sense that the biblical story of Ruth and Orpah, two widowed sisters-in-law, and their mother-in-law, Naomi, offers a compelling model for approaching the question of friendship and "Who's Got My Back?"

At a point of no return in their journeys together, Ruth and Orpah must determine whether they will follow their mother-in-law, with whom they have no connection— no shared culture, no grandchildren—or return to their native land. Ruth is frequently championed for the words of devotion she speaks to Naomi: "Do not entreat me to leave you, or to keep from following you; for wherever you go, I will go; and where you lodge, I will lodge; your people shall be my people, and your God my God."

Orpah's part of the scene often fades, though, although

it is no less significant in helping discover our answers when it comes to questions of connection. Crying, Orpah kisses Naomi and turns to walk a different direction. She knows where she belongs. A later commentary on this text indicates that the kiss Orpah gives Naomi is one of three significant kisses in human existence: the kiss of reunion, the kiss of family, and finally the kiss—Orpah's kiss—of parting. The kiss of parting is another important aspect of a friendship, as opposed to merely the end of one. Whether the parting is chosen by all parties, peoples' lives remain connected forever even when they themselves do not stay friends in perpetuity. They have shared life and therefore are forever a part of one another's. In the Ruth narrative we see two models of having someone's back—one enduring, another episodic, and both invaluable.

Nonetheless, when you find that a friendship has an expiration date it is a heartbreak. In the Gospel of Mark, Peter does not go into the relationship with Jesus believing the friendship will end badly. As he says, "Everyone else may fall away, but I will not." We all build friendships believing this is true. And even though Jesus knows that it has been prophesied that his friends will disown him, he is, nonetheless, unprepared for the force of its reality. With Peter, James, and John at his side, Jesus looks to them for comfort. He pleads, "My heart is ready to break with grief; stop here, and stay awake." But despite their willing spirits, they keep falling asleep; they check out on their friend. And when Peter will not admit he is a friend and disciple of Jesus, even as he hides, he bursts into tears at his own breaking point. The moment is a "Who's Got My Back?" moment—a moment when, as the Fray sing in "Over My Head (Cable Car)," "I'd rather run the other way than stay and see / The smoke and who's still standing when it clears." While Jesus and Peter may have had no choice in their story's outcome because of the larger "script" in which their connection takes place, we do. If we can find a way to stay standing, to see who's still there and who simply cannot be, after a time of intense transition, something will have been revealed that might never have been otherwise.

This is the risk in really determining who's got your back. Your answer will not come without fissures and cracks along the way, without a chasm opening between you and another person. But knowing whether the gap is temporary or permanent, if not necessary, will also help you find your answer to this question. You'll know who is in your life for life, who is in your life for a moment, and how to say good-bye in such a way that you can still inhabit the worlds the friendship inspired, even if your paths won't or can't cross anymore. And when the opportunity arises to let someone new into your life, you'll have all the more time, wisdom, love, and care to offer because of what others have offered you.

All These People

I've never been a huge Prince fan, but on Super Bowl Sunday 2006, I was converted. On that day he was a preacher on a national sacred holiday, kicking off the halftime show with his signature spoken words: "Dearly beloved, we're gathered here to get through this thing called life." He then took the seventy-five-thousand-person crowd in his hands in a driving rain that seemed more than fitting when just days beforehand, a matter of miles away, central Florida residents had lost their homes and their loved ones to a series of tornadoes with angry, destructive, unceasing rhythms. During the stunning finale, which could have been none other than "Purple Rain," the master performer turned master teacher, kicked away his microphone, putting himself and his song in the hands of the people—not just letting them raise their voices, but letting them know that without their voices the song would not go on. It was their turn.

I sensed that Prince knew just what he was doing that night, and not only because he is a musical marvel, but because he was sending another message, consciously, even incorporating the words of the Foo Fighters's 1995 song "Best of You" to ask the crowd a rather poignant question at a critical moment: "Is someone getting the best of you?" And the way he asked, it was anything but rhetorical. He seemed to be asking his congregation of millions whether they were giving their best to at least one person. Because with all of the challenges we're facing as a human community, no one's service, no one's ingenuity, time, talent, intellect, or compassion can be spared.

Now take a moment to wonder, when others ask themselves who's got their back, are you one of the people who come to mind? Is someone "getting the best of you?" Can you pick up the mike and sing for someone else who has no voice because an unceasing rain is falling on his life, beating right through the roof that was supposed to keep her safe and dry? Is someone getting the best *from* you?

It's possible, and a reality you can bring into existence if it isn't already the case, that the people who come to mind won't know your name, wouldn't even be able to recognize your face in a stadium crowd. They may not fall into the category of family or friend, but could be complete strangers. They've got your back, nonetheless, because they, too, bring out another side of you, another world in you, because they need you and what only you can offer. In this spirit, no one is really a stranger.

New Orleans native Harry Connick Jr. and gospel great Kim Burrell sum it up best in their song, "All These People." All of the tune's proceeds go to Hurricane Katrina relief. The lyrics demonstrate how quickly strangers can become neighbors, family even, when life unearths the inherent vulnerability, the hair breadth's distance between comfort and catastrophe in every existence that truly makes us start sentences with the phrase, "There but for the grace of . . ." The pair sing: "I was so damn scared I held hands with a crazy man. . . . We were just brothers that stood there and stared."

"All these people" are the ones whose lives reflect thoroughly possible realities in our own, possibilities that may not stay right in front of our eyes, but are the flip side of the coin—the way it could be, might have been, would be but for a couple clicks of that mysterious dial that sends us into our own particular geographical, socioeconomic, cultural, religious, and temporal little corner of the universe. Perhaps that's what Connick and Burrell are intimating in the same song when they say, "One day a stranger, one day my kin."

As Reverend Martin Luther King Jr. said in a 1965 commencement address he delivered at Oberlin College called "Remaining Awake Through a Great Revolution," "For some strange reason I can never be what I ought to be until you are what you ought to be. And you can never be what you ought to be until I am what I ought to be. This is the way God's universe is made; this is the way it is structured." There is no telling when we'll find a powerful stranger-to-stranger connection that we otherwise would attribute, ideally, to the kind of closeness, responsiveness, and availability we would reserve for family or friends.

And in that mighty human calculus we see ourselves in others whom we might otherwise have looked past or around. In short, it takes an "other" to show us more of the picture of life and how life needs us. When you hear the call of a so-called stranger's life, and know that call is not one to which you can turn your back without losing something of your own potential, you've added another layer to "Who's Got My Back?" It's knowing when, to paraphrase founding father Thomas Paine, "the time—and the person—hath found you." And, in those unexpected points of connection and action, when strangers become neighbors, friends, and family—even if but for a moment, when the people we meet along life's way reach into our souls, compel us to extract the best of who we are and make an offering of it, and do so in a way even a close friend cannot, that we begin to wonder who needed whom more.

Knowing who's got your back is discovering who can draw out the unique flavor of your existence or put the passion back into your purpose, just as you do the same for someone whose life circumstances have drained the delight from living. As Matthew explained, "If salt becomes tasteless, how is its saltness to be restored? It is now good for nothing but to be thrown away and trodden underfoot." But there are no living, breathing human beings who do not possess the salt of the earth—the seasoning they are here to bring to the unique mix of humanity. And just as salt brings out sweetness in baking, you must find your moment to be salt to the world, whether the scale be large or small, to help another person find their flavor again.

That intimacy, as essential as it is unlikely, among strangers and neighbors is detailed with great frequency in the Bible. Readings from Exodus, Leviticus, and Deuteronomy in particular reveal that caring for "our neighbors" requires two elements: (1) that when a person falls on hard times it is as if he has become a member of your household and (2) you must open your heart and your hand to lend "as much as a person lacks, that which he has not." Ancient rabbis wondered about the repetition in the latter obligation (from Deuteronomy) when the two phrases appear to mean the same thing. On this point they taught that "as much as he lacks" means sustaining another person's living, yet not necessarily making him rich. As for "that which he has not," they insisted that having someone's back in a tough time means knowing what a quality life means to them—understanding their definition of what constitutes a home, comfort, substance, joy. The sages offer an example of a prominent scholar who, having discovered a neighbor in need, arranged for two things he knew the man was accustomed to having: a horse and a person to lead him on horseback. The scholar took the responsibility so seriously that he didn't farm out the job to another person, but led the man around on the horse himself for miles at a time, so the man could feel like himself again—so he could have *his* life back.

These ancient teachings remain so radical in a contemporary context because they require not simply that we reach out when someone is in need, but that we understand their needs by getting to know what constitutes a good life in their eyes. The limitations are there: we are not meant to make a person who has become impoverished rich in the monetary sense, but we are meant to understand what once brought richness to his life and to be a part of restoring it—to do no less than help build a person's spirit, seasoning his taste for life when life has left him with no appetite for living. As British rabbi Jonathan Wittenberg teaches in *The Three Pillars of Judaism*, "When something is a human issue it is my issue. Deeper than my definition of myself as a member of my family is my definition of myself as a member of my people; deeper than my definition of myself as a member of my people is my definition of myself as a human being. It is a truism that I hurt in the same way as you hurt." Find the object of your service in the moment when your service is required, and you will find another person who shows you more of who you are. It's easier when it's someone you already know because the points of connection are in place, but the person you know isn't always the one who needs you most. That person who needs you to get his back is inviting you into a partnership that will show you another, once hidden, side of yourself that no "intimate" could—a part that will leave you wondering how you ever lived as long as you did without knowing it was there.

Let's Get Critical

Finding that a stranger can have your back by drawing another facet from your being doesn't always bring the warm fuzzies. In fact, I have heard a daring principle attributed to today's Dalai Lama: "In the practice of tolerance, one's enemy is the best teacher." Someone entirely unknown to you who doesn't know who you are, what makes you hurt, what you need, and, quite possibly, doesn't care, can also have your back in an odd, yet curiously indispensable way. Along these same lines, comedienne Sarah Silverman, whose no-holds-barred approach to humor pushes the boundaries of political correctness, spoke candidly in a 2007 *New York Times* feature about a critic whom she realized had her back, even though they had never met face-to-face. At the time, he was commenting on her 2005 film *Jesus Is Magic*, with its blend of commentary on race, sex, and politics (pretty much all the stuff you're not supposed to discuss at dinner parties or, in Silverman's case, say anywhere, out loud, *ever*). The critic insisted that Silverman's incendiary, politically incorrect comedic approach was actually a form of playing it safe. Upon reading those words Silverman said, "It totally hurt my feelings and was like a kick in the stomach." The reason why it hurt so much was because what the critic was saying, in her own words, "was something that always festered in the back of my mind that I never talked about." She, too, had begun to wonder if she was really pushing boundaries or just pressing buttons that people already were accustomed to having pressed, but it wasn't until her critic articulated that concern that she was able to begin assessing that part of her work in earnest. While it may have been salt in a wound at the time, that voice in the paper helped Silverman surface a question she is still trying to answer with her work, which can only make her a better professional, a more innovative entertainer—the kind she wants to be and has been striving to be for more than twenty of her thirty-six years.

A Jewish maxim highlights this notion: "Do not despise any person, and do not dismiss anything; for there is not a person who doesn't have his hour and there is not one thing that does not have a place [in your life]." It takes the whole Andy Warhol "fifteen minutes of fame" theory in a slightly different direction. Sometimes someone may have your back by being significant in your life long after they've actually passed through it. Suddenly something they said that you didn't even realize you heard will reappear at just the right moment.

I had a professor once whom no one liked all that much. He seemed to enjoy making sport out of cornering people in class, verbally harassing them to the point of embarrassment. Most of what he said made little sense, the stuff of grandstanding more than it was the sharing of grand ideas and sage advice; sitting through the lectures, rather than drawing something of meaning from them, was its own acknowledged rite of passage among the student body. Yet with the class long over, and the professor himself no longer of this earth, one line he offered remains with me to this day and helps me when I'm trying to be there for others. He said, "You don't need to be God's defender." It was that simple. And for that one line, that one insight, I'm forever grateful. Because the last thing a person needs in the face of life's sorrows, in the thick of confounding personal and global injustices, in the suck of everyday setbacks is a person sitting before them to plead the Ruler of the Universe's case. If I only learned one thing that semester I learned one of the most important: we are all here to bear witness to peoples' pain, to support them through it, to try and change what we can, but not to explain it away by making excuses or offering patty-cake platitudes on behalf of an all-powerful being who, if all-powerful, can surely take care of Him- or Herself. We have to take care of one another.

That professor had my back; he still does. I just had to see it. Knowing that this can happen with anyone at any time makes you take care of others, see people in a way that rarely allows for writing anyone off as useless or 100 percent your adversary. And, over time, this awareness can make for a very different kind of world and a different experience of our time in it.

YOUR HIGHLIGHTER

Ready to find your answer? All you have to do is engage your highlighter. As you reflect on this question and the different facets we've explored, notice the things that give you the chills, make you stop and take notice, the reasons why you drive the long way home, what makes you opt for a walk through the park or a ride on your bicycle instead of hopping on the subway or into your car, or leaves you humming the melody to a song you haven't heard in years. If you need a little extra help getting your highlighter in motion, use these additional questions, based on ideas in the chapter, as a jump start.

- Which realm of relationship is driving this question in your life: family, friend, neighbor, stranger?

- What piece of the puzzle of your life is not yet in your possession that a connection with another person might bring out? Where is your blind spot?

- Have you reached a point of connection with another person that needs deepening and development?

- Are you facing a moment of parting, and, if so, how can you carry the connection with you once the good-bye has been said?

- Who needs the "best of you" right now?

- Who is getting the best of you—in the negative sense (i.e., making you doubt yourself, feel drained)—who, seen differently, might have your back for what they can teach you (even if you don't want to have coffee with them!)?

....

Who Has My Heart?

It is only necessary to know that love is a direction and not a state of the soul.

—Simone Weil, *Waiting for God*

If our relationships with friends, family, neighbors, and strangers reveal the substance of who we are and might be, then all the more so with the people we choose to commit ourselves to in intimate, singular, and sustained relationships. Or, as Erich Fromm writes in *The Art of Loving*, "In the act of loving, of giving myself, in the act of penetrating the other person, I find myself, I discover myself, I discover us both, I discover man." The Goo Goo Dolls have a similar version of Fromm's teaching, "I just want you to know who I am."

In years of officiating at weddings, I've learned that this "knowing" takes many forms. It may result in marriage. It may result in more than one marriage. It may mean never marrying at all, but remaining exclusively involved with the same person over time, without a piece of paper of any kind that spells out the details. In whatever form these relationships take, the question of how and to whom you give your heart is one that, if kept alive, not only before but most especially after you have entered into an ongoing commitment, allows you to keep discovering new things in yourself and to be more giving to others.

This chapter and this question are inspired by, but are not about, marriage. "Who Has My Heart?" can be your question whether you've been with the same person for thirty years, are struggling to make a commitment, or are about to take a leap of faith after hitting the ground with a thud many a time when making an offering of the heart to another. You can be asking because you want to know where and in whom to place your trust, you might be asking because you want to recommit yourself to a relationship that has been slowed to a near holding pattern because the tailwinds of time simply aren't enough to move it forward anymore, or this question could be in your life because you're realizing you've never let someone have your heart. Ever.

In any event, an age-old saying attributed to Reb Nachman of Bratslav claims that the only whole heart is a broken one, so letting this question into your life at any point also means knowing that your heart is always in for a workout when you let it open to another person. But it is an essential workout, one without which we live but aren't fully alive. Franz Kafka's short story, "First Sorrow," about a famed trapeze artist so dedicated to his craft that he rarely was comfortable on the ground, highlights our collective reticence, even in long-term and long-tested intimate relationships, to give anyone special access to something that can break so easily. So accustomed was the trapeze artist to living his solitary life in the rafters that when he had to travel, he would situate himself in the luggage rack of the train (difficult given today's carry-on restrictions, odd even by the standards of his time, but then again, this is Kafka!).

The trapeze artist's great moment of crisis comes when he realizes not only that he wants, but that he needs, a second bar—two trapezes for his performances, opposite each other. "Only the one bar in my hands—how can I go on living!" he says. His manager rebukes himself for not having thought of it sooner, for letting the trapeze artist be a solo act for so very long, and yet the manager—because, after all, he is a manager—worries this could be the unraveling of his star performer's career. The manager says, "Once such ideas began to torment him, would they ever quite leave him alone? Would they not rather increase in urgency? Would they not threaten his very existence?"

The trapeze artist, suddenly and startlingly aware that he no longer wants to swing through life alone, has reached a moment of risk far greater than the one he faces each night in his act. It is reminiscent of a moment in Genesis when God finds Adam moping about the Garden of Eden—Eden, where he has everything a person could want and need, everything except for another person. Seeing his suffering, God, like the manager, says, "It is not good for a human being to be alone." And yet, even Adam, who wants to know the very heart of, and be known in his heart by, another person still struggles against her presence when the time comes. According to the story, God, acting as the First Anesthesiologist, puts Adam into a deep sleep so that Eve can come into being. Sure, when he sees her for the first time he knows that she is the person he had been searching for in a Paradise that lacked for paradise. Yet had he been awake for the procedure, even though it was elective, he might have backed out of the whole thing.

And so it is that we, too, resist the unique connection with another person we know we need because it carries the risk of any serious surgery. Hopefully things will turn out for the best, but there are no guarantees. The scene from Terrence McNally's play, *Frankie and Johnny in the*

Clair de Lune, captures that desire for discovering oneself in another and the concomitant desire to retreat when the revelation, no matter how joyous, is like waking and consciously understanding that your chest is open on the table. Frankie, phoning in a request to a local radio station, narrates the highs, the lows, the complications, and the contentment:

> Right off. They both knew tonight was going to happen. So why did it take six weeks for him to ask her if she wanted to see a movie that neither one of them could tell you the name of right now? Why did they eat ice cream sundaes before she asked him if he wanted to come up since they were in the neighborhood? And then they were making love and for maybe an hour they forgot the ten million things that made them think, "I don't love this person. I don't even like them" and instead all they knew was that they were together and it was perfect and they were perfect and that's all there was to know about it and as they lay there, they both began the million reasons not to love one another like a familiar rosary.

The moments of real knowing, when hearts are open, are terrifying and exhilarating, are miraculous in their very occurrence, yet so easily forgotten even minutes later. Perhaps this is why the Jewish sages said that creating a truly intimate, lasting connection between two people is as difficult as dividing the Red Sea. Now that is *the* miracle par excellence—the biggie. Very Hollywood. The not-so-Hollywood moments come after the cool special effects, when the Israelites are complaining that they want to go back to Egypt, despite having their freedom, despite having seen one of the most unbelievable sights known to humanity.

How similar sometimes to our most significant relationships, when we let our hearts open to another person, and that miraculous knowing is so staggering in the moment. Yet it is also frightening to have shared such an extraordinary experience. What of the moments to come? What if you can't find each other again? What happens when you realize that the next time, *you'll* have to make the waters part if you want to keep traveling together?

It's easy to lose the instant of the miracle, when everything is possible. I don't think the rabbis thought it was so difficult to get people together, as much as they knew how hard it might be for them to remember that they experienced a miracle in finding each other to begin with. They knew that people, like the Israelites, lose their openness and gratitude for the mere fact of that miracle so quickly, and then wait for more moments to appear rather than making them happen. Surely the redactors of the Talmud and James Joyce were not in direct conversation with one another, but it seems they could have been. The couple in Joyce's *The Dead*, Gabriel and Gretta, have lost touch with their miracle, and so, too, with each other. Gabriel senses Gretta's distance and her proximity, thinking the words he somehow cannot say out loud as he watches her walk a few paces ahead of him on a cold January night: "Like the tender fire of stars moments of their life together, that no one knew of or would ever know of, broke upon and illumined his memory. He longed to recall to her those moments, to make her forget the years of their dull existence together and remember only their moments of ecstasy. . . . In one letter that he had written to her then he had said: 'Why is it that words like these seem to me so dull and cold? Is it because there is no word tender enough to be your name?'"

Even as Gabriel struggles to communicate with the one person whom it should be the easiest to talk to, he recalls a place from their courtship, a place beyond words. That place is the heart.

Heart Monitor

In Homer's *Odyssey*, Penelope waits some twenty years for her love, Odysseus, to return from battle. No one believes he is still alive, yet Penelope insists that he is.

When she can no longer keep the eager, traitorous suitors at bay in his absence, she devises a plan to buy her more time: she takes up knitting. Penelope makes it known that she has begun a knitting project for her father-in-law and that she cannot consider any of the enthusiastic gents hanging about her house until she has completed it. So she knits by day and unravels her work by night.

Finally, Odysseus returns from Troy. Yet the two do not share words at their reunion. She tries to explain to her son, Telemachus, how she will know that the man who has returned is Odysseus, indeed. She says:

> If he really is Odysseus, truly home,
> beyond all doubt we two shall know each other
> better than you or anyone. There are
> secret signs we know, we two.

And once the two have reunited, she adds, "You make my hardened heart know that I am yours."

So what is this heart-speak? What does it mean for someone to have your heart, to know you in such a way that your connection runs deeper than any words, let alone saying, "I love you" when that phrase can mean many different things to different people? A Valentine's Day cover of the *New Yorker* magazine illustrated these differences notion perfectly, depicting people sitting on a subway with cartoon balloon captions rising from their heads. Each one portrayed separate universes of thought on love: A man dreams of walking hand-in-hand with the woman sitting near him, as that same woman, clasping a book that appears to be called *An Angel Among Derelicts*, simultaneously imagines him with flies coming out of his hair and clothes (i.e., *not* feeling the love!). A woman with a crying baby in a stroller daydreams of walking through the park next to the nice person seated next to her, but his fantasy balloon has a stroller with a big X through it. Also on the cover, two people holding on to the same metal pole are actually thinking of each other sharing a romantic candlelit dinner. Yet one imagines a *Romeo and Juliet* balcony scene, and the other, *Casablanca*. They are all on the same page, but they are not.

My friend Elli once misquoted a U2 song, "The Original of the Species," as we talked about how difficult it is for peoples' hearts to speak to one another in the same language when we're all these complex universes in and unto ourselves. He said, "The end is not as far as the start," meaning, it's harder to make an initial, meaningful connection that has lasting potential. As it turned out, the line of the song is, "The end is not as fun as the start." I have to admit, I liked Elli's interpretation of the lyrics better.

That heart connection is like a prayer. Not because it's

something you have to pray for, but in the sense that the first time a prayer is uttered in the Bible, the literal translation of what the person is doing is "speaking to his heart." So what does it mean for someone to have your heart? Two things: In order for someone else to have your heart, you must first "have" yours by learning how to speak to it and by becoming fluent in what it has to say to you. As you develop your ability to scan your heart and know it well, you'll also become aware of the things your heart will only tell you when you're in partnership with another person—the things that are beyond words, and yet are as accessible to you as your native tongue when a person who speaks the language of your heart enters your life.

If you know your heart well, you will be able to see how it functions with different people. A person who has your heart can hear and see and draw out things you may not have known were there, but with which you'll feel unusually familiar once they've been uncovered. And while there isn't only one person in the world capable of talking to your heart in this way, there aren't scores of those people, either. Becoming fluent in the language of your own heart will let you know when those rare some-ones appear. If you choose the connection and commit to deepening it, it can be like letting someone hear your deepest prayer. Or, as Marilyn and Alan Bergman put it in their beautiful lyrics to "What Are You Doing the Rest of

Your Life," "When you stand before the candles on a cake / Oh let me be the one to hear the silent wish you make."

Changes

Because we're always changing, a person who has your heart is someone with whom you can change and vice versa. In this sense the "having" is not a possession, but an infinite direction where neither you nor the other person needs to control what goes on in each other's hearts to share them.

One of my all-time favorite love stories in the Torah (not that there is vast competition for the title) is that of Isaac and Rebecca because the two are not simply locked in a predestined, preordained, orchestra-swelling romance, but in an enduring and uncommon knowing that holds all the mysterious elements of any intimate relationship: luck, attraction, friendship, timing, and choice. Isaac and Rebecca are, for all intents and purposes, the precursor to eHarmony.com. By all accounts, they are a match quite literally made in heaven and excellent on paper—shared background, shared interests (not that shepherding is likely among eHarmony's compatibility match criteria). At any rate, that person—the first one to pray and speak to his heart—well, he was the match-maker, sent by Isaac's father, Abraham, to find the right woman for his son. Humbled by a task so great, he prayed that certain signs would let him know precisely who that woman was, so he wouldn't fall down on the job when the time came. He asked that the woman in question be the first to offer water to his camel when he rested from his journey, and she did. He asked that she invite him to share in her family's hospitality, and she did. Everything he asked for in the way of a sign happened. Should've been a done deal, right?

However, on the order of miracles, something truly miraculous by biblical standards occurs in this tale. No seas part, no thunder claps, no heavens rain manna. But a wonder of a different sort occurs, one that we can experience to this day. Even though Rebecca, Isaac's mate-to-be, has heard the story, even though her father has declared that this match has the fingerprints of the Divine all over it, one critical question must be asked before Rebecca packs her things. With Abraham's servant in a mad rush to get Rebecca to Isaac, Rebecca's family decides to ask her what she wants to do. "Will you go with this man?" they ask (in a television show, this would be the moment where they'd cut to a commercial). Everything can change in that instant, and you can feel everyone holding their breath. Until, finally, Rebecca says, "I will go."

I invoke this mix of that which is bigger than us and that which we must choose when people are just about to stand under their wedding canopies. Even after the traditional wedding contract and civil license have been signed, and before the ceremony itself, I ask each partner to answer that same question: Will you go with this man? Will you go with this woman? I tell them it will be their job to keep asking themselves in the days and years to come, to keep choosing to give each other their hearts.

I think Milos Forman, in his role as Father Havel in 2000's *Keeping the Faith*, offers one of the clearest descriptions of how crucial constant choosing is in any intimate relationship that has our hearts. I'll confess that I didn't want to see this movie when it came out. I was a rabbinical student at the time, and I had (and still have) this thing about the way people in the clergy are usually portrayed in film and television. Typically they're not shown as real people who say real things or feel real human feelings, such as confusion, doubt, or despair. The most they tend to do is offer a "Dearly beloved, we are gathered here today" or they're merely seen "tsk-tsk-tsking" at everyone, from a captive congregation to the casual passerby. But my close friend and fellow seminary student talked me into it with the argument that the movie would be cause for conversation and that we should at least have an informed opinion. Well, I loved *Keeping the Faith*. Furthermore, as penance for having been such a naysayer, it's my duty to reveal that the following scene held so much truth for me that it brought me to tears. Here, the elder Father Havel counsels his young charge, Father Brian (played by Ed Norton), who is reconsidering his decision to enter the priesthood. Father Havel says: "The truth is you can never tell yourself there is only one thing you could be. If you're a priest, or if you marry a woman, it's the same challenge. You cannot make a real commitment unless you accept that it's a choice that you keep making again and again and again."

This film moment reminded me of an ancient allegory that builds off the story of the revelation of the Law at Mount Sinai. A rabbi says that God picked up the mountain and held it over the people, basically making them an offer they can't refuse—if, that is, they want to live—saying (roughly), "If you accept, it's all good; if not, this will be your burial place." This kind of "choosing" is not a choice, though—not the kind that will hold your heart, and not the kind you want someone else's heart in. Love is a choice you make, a direction you take through action every single day—not out of desperation or the fear that comes with the threat of losing what's safe, but through the deep, abiding, not entirely explicable language of the heart that keeps people connected to one another in life, rather than in a life sentence.

Only you can give your heart, and only you can know with whom it should be shared in a singular fashion, shared with someone who knows that being there is standing on sacred ground. I referred to a Marilyn and Alan Bergman song earlier, and the two who've been together for fifty years, have a thing or twelve to teach about how to see the question, "Who Has Your Heart?" One of the best is in another song they wrote, whose title is also a question: "How Do You Keep the Music Playing?" It has been sung by many a great, including my personal favorite, Barbra Streisand. But the James Ingram and Patti Austin duet, from the movie for which this tune was the Academy Award–winning title track, 1982's *Best Friends* with Goldie Hawn and Burt Reynolds, is probably the best-known rendition. Hawn and Reynolds play professional screenwriters who have lived and worked together for many years and decide to get married as an afterthought. As they say, "hijinks ensue," including a wonderfully memorable high-stress lunch with the new mother-in-law during which Goldie Hawn does a valium-induced face plant into her chicken salad. Nonetheless, it isn't until the couple chooses each other again, under changed circumstances, aware that they'll never know for certain whether their hearts will be safe, but knowing that the other is the only one they want to chance their hearts with, that they are really linked for life. And so the Bergmans offer their answer, and perhaps theirs will inspire your own: "If we can try with every day to make it better as it grows, with any luck, then I suppose, the music never ends."

Who has your heart? Rabbi David Wolpe once said in a lecture that, besides God (if you believe in God), the only person who can ever really have your heart, who can know you from the inside-out, is you; that someone can be physically inside of you and still never know how it feels to be you. But if you know your heart well, if you really keep your own lines of connection open to talking to and hearing it, the person or people who you'll work hardest to share that secret language with are the ones who'll have it, too.

Y O U R   H I G H L I G H T E R

These questions, based on the focus question in the chapter, are here to help you find your answer. If you're noticing that you're responding to certain peoples' stories with greater interest, are hitting "repeat" on a particular song on your iPod, or are finding you don't like a certain movie you once would have been thrilled to catch by accident on one of the four hundred cable channels you have that never show anything good, these are all examples of your highlighter in action—pointing you to what you know.

- What is driving this question in your life? Is it a relationship you're already in, one you hope to find, or the feeling that you're ready to ask yourself the question for the first time?

- Do you have a way of talking to your heart?

- Is there someone who you know, based on your own "heart-talks," who can speak your heart's language, even if what your heart is saying is something you've never heard it say before?

- Who is the person who shows you the most of yourself, has been the best surprise you never saw coming but can't imagine your life without?

- Who is the person who you don't want to change, but want to change with?

What's It All About?

Prior: The point, dear, the point . . .
Louis: That it should be the questions and shape of a life,
its total complexity gathered, arranged and considered,
which matters in the end . . .

—Tony Kushner, *Angels in America*

Jazz legend Billie Holliday and composer Arthur Herzog wrote two songs together over the course of their respective lives, both of which remain legendary to this day. The ballad "Strange Fruit" pulses with the unrealized possibilities of every hanged African-American citizen whose killers thought their crimes could go unpunished because their victims' lives were worth less than their own. "God Bless the Child" is its own cry for social responsibility, yet it is a cry with the gentle cadence of a lullaby. The refrain is "Papa may have / Mama may have / but God bless the child that's got his own." As the words suggest, you have to find your reasons for being here.

If you're reading this chapter, it's likely you're reading it in concert with at least one other in this book. And that makes a great deal of sense. Because every single question driving our lives in a particular moment is always driven by another question: What's It All About? Although we may not be aware of it at the time, the way we answer all the other questions in and with our lives shapes a system of beliefs that make us who we aspire to be in word and who we struggle to become in deed. "What's It All About?" is another way of asking, "What really matters to me, and how does the meaning I ascribe to those things affect the way I act in the world?" This question blinks like a cursor on every single page of the stories we write with our lives, until there are no blank pages left. As pioneering psychiatrist and Holocaust survivor Viktor Frankl wrote in *Man's Search for Meaning*, "Ultimately man should not ask what the meaning of life is, but rather must recognize that it is he who is asked. In a word, each man is questioned by life, and he can only answer to life by answering for his own life; to life he can only respond by being responsible." Put simply, our jobs aren't to determine the meaning of life, but to make our lives meaningful.

Life is a question, and you are an answer. But you can't be an answer before you have a context, can't "get your own" until you get what's come before you. Something larger than ourselves constantly informs our experiences, gives us roots in the shifting sands of the everyday, and helps us make meaning of and in the world. In *Acts of Meaning*, psychologist Jerome Bruner calls this "agentivity." He explains that by placing ourselves within a larger story, as opposed to standing apart from it, we can direct our actions more effectively toward our goals. By knowing the larger stories in which we place our lives and our faith—really, just another way of saying "trust"—we know ourselves better and can achieve more with that knowledge.

I'd like to say that I learned what Bruner meant from the man himself, but actually a New York City cab driver ended up being my best teacher. Taped to the divider between the front and backseat of the cab was a piece of paper with the driver's handwriting. I quickly grabbed a scrap of paper of my own and over the potholes and sudden stops at missed traffic lights, wrote down everything on that sheet, word for word: Deuteronomy 6:4–9, Jeremiah 29:11–14, Leviticus 20:26, Matthew 22:37–38, John 14:6–7. At the bottom of his piece of paper, the driver had inscribed, "God's word."

Regardless of whether you call the Bible the "Old Testament" or the "New Testament," whether you call yourself "religious," "spiritual," or "secular," you know there's more to what some identify as "God's word," than those five short passages. But the list was the story in which this man had chosen to plant his life and from which he was trying to direct his purpose, his values, and his commitments. Those verses were his agentivity.

Oftentimes how we wrestle with the question of what we believe, rather than the consistency of those beliefs, creates the most compelling and inspiring contours of our lives. And finding a context for that struggle gives us a sense of rootedness, even if the larger stories in which we place our lives—whether they be religious, historical, political, familial, cultural, or some combination of them all— are the very stories we are rejecting because who we are and what we face now compels us to find new beliefs.

Sunday School Dropout

Of course it's nearly impossible to talk about what it's all about without religion entering the conversation. Even if you would never call yourself a religious person, it's out there. So, let's deal with it first. Many, many definitions in Latin and Middle English attempt to trace the etymology of "religion." One, in particular, breaks the word into two, from the Latin: *re*, meaning "to return," and *ligare*, meaning "to bind." Or, as *Webster's Collegiate Dictionary* offers, religion means "return to bondage." Another definition comes from Cicero. He also thought the word to be derived from the Latin *relegere*, meaning "to read again."

Putting the particular framework of any one religion aside, when we consider "What's It All About?" we are really at the junction between that to which we bind our lives and that which we must constantly examine—or "read again." There comes a point in all of our lives when what we once believed, when what we thought was unshakeable, does not hold anymore. In these moments, we must free ourselves from the bonds of old ideas no longer capable of being worthy vessels for our lives, and read again—either to add new or renewed meaning to a long-held belief, or to put our trust in something we never could have seen or known until that moment.

On the eve of her 2007 induction into the Rock and Roll Hall of Fame, punk rock doyenne Patti Smith wrote of her own "religious" awakening in a special *New York Times* op-ed. She describes a life-altering experience of undeniably strong connection that shaped her life (and, by extension, the lives of others) that could only come into being with a break with a tradition equally as strong:

> On a cold morning in 1955, walking to Sunday school, I was drawn to the voice of Little Richard wailing "Tutti Frutti" from the interior of a local boy's makeshift

clubhouse. So powerful was the connection that I let go of my mother's hand.

Rock 'n' roll. It drew me from my path to a sea of possibilities.

Smith captured an aspect of what happens when we connect with what we really believe, as opposed to forcing connections with what we believe we should think. As a person who has studied, and studies, my own religion extensively, and as someone who also enjoys learning about the religious traditions of others, I find that religions always come into being in some revolutionary way—with an idea or a set of ideas that, at first, are a rejection of existing constraints. It is only when the break occurs that new ties emerge. All of the great religious narratives chronicle peoples' transformations, not their static observance and unchallenged devotion from day one to the last day of their lives. Why, then, do we associate religion with being bound, restrained, unchanging, and constrained? Why should we not all, whether in its context or without, be given the same opportunity to live a story—just as Jesus, Moses, Muhammed, and other luminaries did? Whatever you call yourself, however you identify, you cannot live any practice unless—and until—you live. Your life is an original, and therefore, if your struggles and revelations are denied—whether you deny them for yourself, or submit to denying them—the world is denied the wisdom of your struggle.

You don't have to reject everything you've inherited. You don't have to let go of the hand that led you to the place you are now. But, if you want it—if you want anything upon which you build your life, for that matter—genuinely to be yours, you must claim it with your whole being. In the words of the German philosopher Goethe, quoted by Schopenhauer, "What you have inherited from your forefathers you must first win for yourself if you are to possess it." No matter what, you'll have to get your own. For, as Rabbi Abraham Joshua Heschel, who walked arm-in-arm with Reverend Martin Luther King Jr. for civil rights, wrote in *Who Is Man?*:

> My existence as an event is an original, not a copy. No two human beings are alike. A major mode of being human is uniqueness. Every human being has something to say, to think, or to do which is unprecedented.

In the spirit of Heschel, Goethe, and Cicero who saw the study and observance of religion as an entrepreneurial enterprise, the words of a famous spiritual I'm sure you'll know come to mind: "Gimme That Old-Time religion." As it turns out, though, the song was not originally called "Gimme That Old-Time Religion." In 1891 native

Southerner Charlie D. Tillman published his version of a song he heard while attending an African American church tent meeting in South Carolina. Tillman was so taken with the tune that he adapted the song, and it quickly took hold as a standard in white congregations. But before Tillman put his own flourishes on the tune, it was called "*My* Old Time Religion."

So many with pulpits today—whether they be in houses of worship, on television, radio, or blogs—emphasize a certain communal cohesiveness they believe is the path to collective responsibility. They are the standard-bearers for a perceived, and in most cases well-intentioned, corrective on a society comprised of individuals far too interested in themselves and their own lives (read: narcissism), and, as such, they preach against people bringing My Space language into the development of their beliefs. I heard a learned and well-respected colleague, for instance, talk of his disdain for those who use the phrase "my Judaism" to describe their connection to and expression of their equal portion of inherited Jewish wisdom, ritual, and tradition—ostensibly asserting there is no such thing as *my* old-time religion, but only "that old-time religion." This same colleague, however, went on to utilize the very phrase he claimed to find sick-making to characterize his own understanding of what it means to be and to act as a Jew in the world today. There is no such thing as "*that* old-time religion," unless you're interested in that system being preserved like a shriveled rose pressed between the pages of an old Bible worn from someone else's use and now kept as a family heirloom. As German theologian Meister Eckhart claimed in a sermon entitled "I Have Chosen You": "That I am a man I have in common with all men; that I see and hear and eat and drink I share with all animals; but that I am I is exclusively mine, and belongs to no one but myself." Unless there is a "my" in the equation, that which is exclusively yours, which calls to you from that greater wisdom, you'll have something to take out on special occasions, admire, sigh wistfully, even, and then wrap back up in tissue paper for safekeeping until the next scheduled viewing. In the meantime you have a life to lead. And you can't build a life with tissue paper.

However, if you acquire your own "What's It All Abouts," regardless of whether they make sense from the outside to anyone else looking in, you will feel less concerned with your own beliefs shifting and being challenged over time. According to the Popol Vuh, the creation story in Mayan religion, many attempts were made in the effort to make the first human beings. The final attempt, which resulted in what the story calls "true people," was the construction of humans with maize—their flesh consisting of white and yellow corn. That combination of white and yellow corn is the mixture of what we inherit and what we create, what we leave aside and what we acquire anew. If we stop looking for uniformity and consistency in the imperfect, evolving systems we receive, we will also stop looking for that same uniformity over the course of what, hopefully, are full and colorful lives of our own, including particularly definitive moments when we must, by circumstance and conviction, change direction—when what it's all about is something different than what it was before.

In this sense we also become less invested in imposing our beliefs on others, which is, in the final accounting, a strong human communal act. For as civil rights champion Reverend William Sloane Coffin, author of *Passion for the Possible*, said in an oft-quoted note of penetrating insight, "We can build a community out of seekers of truth, but not out of possessors of truth." When we acknowledge that, even as we know, we also seek, we are more humble, yet are no less effective or dedicated for that humility. A scene from novelist Zadie Smith's *White Teeth* illustrates this notion in a way that has stayed as seared in my own being since I read it as any teaching from the Torah or Talmud. The book details the lives of a Bangladeshi family living in England, their struggles with tradition, culture, belief, and assimilation. In this particularly brilliant moment, a son, Millat, has joined a group of Bangladeshi British teens who decide to embrace and express their heritage by burning books in public. Millat gets caught up in the frenzy, as the works of Socrates, Protagoras, Ovid, D. H. Lawrence, Aleksandr Solzhenitsyn, and Nabokov make their way onto the "funeral pyre" of ideas. Watching them burn for their crimes of "blasphemy," Millat acknowledges that he has never read any of the works himself. While the chaos ensues, Millat's mother, Alsana, catches her son on the local news. She is mortified, and engages in her own act of civil disobedience:

> When Millat came home that evening, a great bonfire was raging in the back garden. All his secular stuff— four years' worth of cool pre- and post-Raggastani, every album, every poster, special-edition T-shirts, club flyers collected and preserved over two years, beautiful Air Max sneakers, copies 20–75 of *2000 AD* magazine, signed photo of Chuck D, impossibly rare copy of Slick Rick's "Hey Young World," *The Catcher in the Rye*, his guitar, *The Godfather I* and *II*, *Mean Streets*, *Rumble-fish*, *Dog Day Afternoon*, and *Shaft in Africa*—all had been placed on the funeral pyre, now a smoldering mound of ashes, which was giving off fumes of plastic and paper, stinging the boy's eyes, which were already filled with tears.

"Everyone has to be taught a lesson," Alsana had said, lighting the match with heavy heart some hours earlier. "Either everything is sacred or nothing is. And if he starts burning other peoples' things, then he loses something sacred also."

As you wrestle with "What's It All About?" remember that if many truths exist in an ever-unfolding universe, many truths also are unfolding in you. In your certainty and in your confusion, everything is sacred.

Commanding Voices

Learning what it's all about for you requires developing and honing a commanding voice. The word *commandment* also requires some exploration to make this question a maximally powerful one. People often associate being commanded with God—with a transcendent, omniscient, omnipotent Being who tells you what to do. And within the realm of discussions of commandments, ten get top billing. And, as others say in a way they believe is quite clever and brand-new, to drive those big ten home, "They aren't called the Ten Suggestions." That is true. But those particular ones are not called The Ten Commandments, either. *The Ten Commandments* is a Charlton Heston movie. In Hebrew, those famous ten—the stuff of end-less social debate—are actually called the "ten utterances" or "the ten words." And, in fact, at least in Jewish life, they are ten of 613 other obligations, many of which cannot be upheld today—either because they involve service in the Holy Temple in Jerusalem (which was destroyed in the year 70 CE and is not due for reconstruction until the days of the Messiah); or because they've been stricken from the record, so to speak, due to their irrelevance or downright cruelty as determined over the passage of time (stoning a rebellious child in public is one example that springs to mind).

On the order of obligations, it has always struck me as strange that what would seem to be the most important law in the Torah, in the Book of Deuteronomy, involves the heart: that "you should love the Lord your God with all your heart, with all your soul, with all your being." It seems that if religion were so focused on belief in God that the one thing neither God nor an intelligent group of humans would decree is something as difficult to define, if not impossible to legislate, as love—that it would not leave such a pivotal obligation to the intermittently exuberant, indifferent, raging, and broken human machinery that is the heart. A Hasidic teaching attributed to Rabbi Menachem Mendl of Kotzk comments on the use of the heart in this instance as well, wondering why the verse that follows says, "And all these words I command you this day shall be upon your heart." Why "upon" your heart and not *in* it? Because, the commentary continues, a great mixture of things hover over the heart, but there are only certain things in singular moments to which the heart will open and allow a place of residence. Think about it. Can you feel something before you're ready to feel it? Can you truly know something, learn anything lasting, before you're ready to learn it?

In *A Theologico-Political Treatise* theologian Benedict Spinoza discussed such a phenomenon, which he called a form of piety, yet a piety without dogma. Instead, he defined the elements of belief that shape our lives as those which "stir up the heart to obey." What stirs your heart to obey? This is a very different concept of what it means to be commanded. Whether the obligation has first come from without or has been created from within, that the heart—a tricky customer that doesn't always come right out and tell us what's inside of it—calls for us to obey and tells us that we must find and take hold of those things that summon us to action. Commandedness does not, in fact, begin with a command, but with a question if any commandment has a chance of assuming the force of obligation in our lives.

In this regard, I turn to what I'll call the Burt Bacharach school of Spinoza-style piety. When you read the title of this chapter—What's It All About?—what was the first word that came to mind? Whether you saw the Michael Caine 1966 movie original or the Jude Law remake, it's likely you added "Alfie" as a reflex. This may be the ultimate question—what stirs your heart, what lives at the foundation of what you believe and guides how you attempt to live your beliefs? Bacharach's lyrics to the theme song for *Alfie* don't leave you hanging. They suggest a rather practical way of thinking about this question that extends to all of our lives: "I believe in love, Alfie. Without true love we just exist, Alfie."

Bacharach's answer is true love. That's what it's all about when he boils it down and serves up his elixir of life's meaning in its purest form. Now, I'm not encouraging you to quit your day job and take up songwriting (unless, of course, you believe it's your calling), but I am saying that asking this particular question will begin to help you get to what it is about for you now. If you need inspiration, put the song on your iPod, sing it at a karaoke bar (preferably among good friends, or, alternatively, a roomful of total strangers), but make it real. If your answer to this question is—like Burt's—"love," you'll know that love is the headlining act that stirs your heart to action. And, with that knowledge, you can actively create a life that is an expression of that answer. So, too, if your answer is something else: social justice, family, patriotism, intellectual rigor, tradition, change. And when your answer changes, the power in the question itself will help you redirect your course, reprioritize your time, reimagine how you see yourself, and light your way to how you hope to be seen.

Woody Allen's *Annie Hall* opens with a troubled little boy, Alvy Singer, seated in a psychiatrist's office, his exasperated mother by his side. He has stopped doing his homework and is depressed. Alvy's mother reveals that the behavior began when Alvy read something and learned that the universe is expanding. Ever since, we learn from this scene, he has been focused on the notion that if the universe is expanding, one day it will "break apart." This causes him a great deal of worry. Making no progress with the shrink, Alvy's mother jumps in with a "diagnosis" of her own. "What has the universe got to do with it?" she cries. "You're here in Brooklyn! Brooklyn is not expanding!"

Alvy's mother may not have liked it, but the boy was already in the process of developing his answer for what it's all about. Neurotic tendencies toward envisioning disaster scenarios aside, Alvy's commanding voice, the thing that stirs his heart to action, is a sense of the world beyond his world—that life exists beyond Brooklyn, and that he is a part of that. And while none of Allen's characters have ever been Norman Rockwell portraits (unless

Rockwell did an analyst's office), they have been completely honest in their depictions of the human struggle to make our time worthwhile while we're here.

From Alfie to Alvy, when you find your "about," you develop a more conscious, committed understanding of what you're striving for, what and why you're building, what you want to sustain and be a part of, how to act in ways that reflect what you want your life to mean and where you want it to go. And if your answer makes you stand out, makes you vulnerable to the criticism of others, or leaves you feeling lost in self-doubt, if it is truly *your* answer, you'll possess the strength from the inside out to remind you that you're on the right path.

Yet how can you tell the difference between your true commanding voice at any given moment—an expression of real obligation for you—and that little something that tells you to perform a magical act? Those little somethings like tossing a penny in a well, making a wish on a stray eyelash, and blowing out the candles on your birthday cake all in one breath? (I won't even go into the complex machinations behind those e-mail chains that sweetly threaten that none of your wishes will come true unless you cyber-indenture twenty-five of your best friends into superstitious servitude.) These are insurance policies, mostly harmless ones at that. And while they can't really hurt, doing them does not tell us any more about what it's all about for us unless we understand what beats at the heart of those wishes. Yes, we'll know our desires, but if we go further we can see if they're connected to more than just a want of the moment—if they're linked to a greater longing that is part of a wish you must will to fulfill with your life.

A 2007 *New York Times* article on the power of superstition and magical thinking brought this "insurance policy" mechanism into full relief. Studies by social scientists suggest that many young people begin learning about faith right around the time they start to give up on wishing. Jacqueline Woolley, a professor of psychology at the University of Texas interviewed for the piece, said, "The point at which the culture withdraws support for belief in Santa and the Tooth Fairy is about the same time it introduces children to prayer." Woolley continues, "The mechanism is already there, kids have already spent time believing that wishing can make things come true, and they're just losing faith in the efficacy of that." This does not, I believe, negate the efficacy of prayer, but rather, highlights an innate drive to express our wishes and our hopes in some concrete way. In so doing, we are reminded of those hopes, and may be more inclined to deliver the results ourselves in the meantime (and, for many, without losing sight of the notion that forces greater than ourselves may be at work in the process and progress of those hopes).

Regardless, everything can't be magic. Replacing the Tooth Fairy with a personal wishing well won't cut it when things get tough. When LeBron James kisses the tattoos on each of his wrists before he shoots a free-throw (one for his mother and one for his girlfriend), he still has to make the clutch shot. You might not wash your favorite team's jersey if they're on a winning streak. But what do you do when you're on a losing streak, and none of your tricks are working—not even your lucky socks? The things you will rely upon then come from a larger story that does not depend on the outcome of just one moment. It's rooted more deeply than that. It's the long view in an instant when all you can see is what is directly in front of you. If you've developed a commanding voice that knows what it's all about for you, it will give you the strength to say, "I must," when the easier response is, "I can't." It will be so much a part of you that even when your best insurance policies fail to bring you the clarity of vision you desire, you'll still possess clarity of action.

If you wish for the love or devotion of one person in particular, while that wish indeed may have everything to do with that individual, it also may be an outgrowth of something you hold sacred—of a commitment that unfolds over time, of a clear sense that a meaningful life means having a person to walk through life with. And if that exact wish doesn't come true, you'll still know what you're searching for, and knowing what you're searching for makes it much easier to recognize it when it's as close to you as your own eyelash. If you have a ritual before big games or important presentations, while the buzzer may sound before you've taken your best shot and the presentation may be your professional equivalent of an air ball, you'll know that underneath it is a passion to do your absolute best, to feel that you have given your all, to know at the end of the day that you couldn't have done it better, and that you want to turn the bad day into a stretch of good ones.

What's it all about? Love? Devotion? Passion? Excellence? Find what lives at the very source of your greatest wishing well, and you'll know what it's all about. You'll know the values of your life—not "values" in the amorphous, buzzword sense that the word is often used today, but where you *place* real value in your life. You'll know where the power lies in your commanding voice—not the one you think you should have, but the one you honestly possess. That voice can cheer you, inspire you, override exhaustion, disappointment, cynicism, and pain. It is the voice that moves you to action.

Walking the Line

If commandment is, at least in some part, an internal spark that stirs your heart to action, then no one is a "nonbeliever." Again, this is a term so often associated solely with religion. Yet with so much for our lives to be "about," we all believe in something, whether it finds expression in a structure we've inherited or through one we've built. So the opposite of being a believer is not being a nonbeliever, but rather, being indifferent. Our old friend—"the man tired of life in dispute with his soul"—from ancient Egypt (and the chapter on fear) said it best, "My Soul replies not / Indeed worse than anger is indifference." When the soul does not respond to life's questions, when the heart does not stir, we're lost. When we're angry, rejecting, wrestling with what we thought we knew to be true, we are certainly uncomfortable, but we're also alive.

Perhaps she did not have this particular interpretation in mind when she wrote the song, but a verse from June Carter Cash's "I Walk the Line," reflects the connection between developing a commanding voice and how that development can guide our actions. Johnny Cash, of course, sings the words most famously: "Because you're mine, I walk the line."

Because you're mine, I walk the line. Because these are the words that have sunk into my heart, the commandments that call out to me from within, I walk the line. Once you know what you're commanded to do, you'll know how you want to live out those commands. Each time you do so, you make a pilgrimage.

The Hebrew words for pilgrimage are *aliyat regel*—"raising a foot, or leg." In the ancient sense, Israelite pilgrimage meant people of all backgrounds coming from every part of the land of Israel to Jerusalem three times a year. Yet in a more literal sense of the definition, pilgrimage is what gets you on your feet, oftentimes without even having to think about it; pilgrimage is what moves you, what you stand for. It's what makes you walk the line.

Those reasons for making pilgrimage, for rising to your feet—whether literally or figuratively, can vary over the course of a lifetime. In fact, what leads you to your acts of pilgrimage may have multiple meanings all at once. As Rabbi Nathan said of his dear teacher, Reb Nachman of Bratslav, "Indeed, for all the things he did he never had a single reason, but rather thousands and tens of thousands of deep and elevated motivations—most especially so for this great journey to the Land of Israel."

Pilgrimage is a vital part of many world religions. My friend Seamus told me about the largest one in the world, called the Khumba Mela (Sanskrit words for "jar" and "mixture," respectively). The Khumbha Mela takes place every three years on a rotating basis in different cities in India, with an even bigger gathering once every twelve. This festival marks an ancient struggle between gods and demons over a jar containing the nectar of eternal life. In their struggle, the jar was shaken. And so it is that the Khumba Mela pilgrimages take place in each locale where the struggle is said to have forced a drop of immortality to fall. And it is in those places, where people of all different backgrounds, levels of study, ages, and stations in life share drops of their own wisdom with one another. The places of struggle—not of the triumph of the divine over the demonic—mark the territory for the most diverse convocation of humanity on the planet.

This whole enterprise of living is a pilgrimage on the order of the Khumba Mela: a convergence of committed but not cohesive people in a universe of competing truths and ideals. Even in our own beings, the travel over time to every new place and the return to those places that are familiar reveals a struggle to know what we stand for and how far we're willing to go to keep rising to our feet, to walk the line in our lives each and every day.

In a perfect world, asking what it's all about is a gift every human being should possess. Yet in a broken world, it's a luxury. That is why those of us who have the ability to ask, wonder, search, and find our paths and our truths must do so passionately—not only for our own sake, but for the world's. "The last of the human freedoms," to quote Frankl again from *Man's Search for Meaning*, "[is] to choose one's attitude in any given set of circumstances, to choose one's own way."

Part of choosing our own way, discerning what it's all about, also means losing our way. But getting lost doesn't have to mean disappearing—it can also point to being found. My stepmom unwittingly led me to this awareness when she gave me her well-worn copy of Tom Wolfe's *The Electric Kool-Aid Acid Test* when I was sixteen. Two lines from the book, spoken by Ken Kesey, hung out in my brain, resurfacing seventeen years later when I needed them most: "You're either on the bus or you're off the bus. If you're on the bus, and you get left behind, then you'll find it again."

As long as you keep asking "What's It All About?" you'll never get left behind. And while it can be overwhelming to face the many possible answers we might generate over the course of a lifetime, to acknowledge how much of what we believe can change as we change, if you trust the question—and yourself—it is also freeing. Not only because it means life is still calling and that you still have something to do, something to say, but also because you can take comfort in the notion that we are all struggling with the same questions; that we are, as the Quaker theologian Isaac Penington wrote, "walking sweetly and harmoniously together in the midst of different practices." Or riding the same bus.

YOUR HIGHLIGHTER

Don't forget, you have an internal highlighter that can guide you naturally to your answers. When you stop to listen more carefully than usual to what someone is saying, when you find that you are drawn to a particular book title or magazine article, discover a new interest, perhaps one that surprises you, or you're noticing you've begun to change the way you spend your time, your highlighter is in motion, moving across the pages of life and hinting at the things that are true for you. These questions, based on the different angles of "What's It All About?" we've explored are here to help kick your highlighter into action. Trust your highlighter. Even when you think it's taking you someplace unfamiliar, it's leading you closer to what you know.

- What belief are you trying to acquire right now? What stands between you and making that belief your own?

The Answer

- Are you trying to live your life by a set of "abouts" that you have not yet claimed for yourself? What are the "abouts" you know are yours? What are the "abouts" you believe should be yours? If you set aside the shoulds, what would take their place?

- Without judging why, what stirs your heart to action? What are your heart's commandments?

- What will you "walk the line" for?

....

Am I Missing Something?

*I am blind and I know nothing, but I see
there are more ways to go; and everything
is an infinity of things.*

—Jorge Luis Borges, "The Unending Rose"

In April 2007, for one frightening forty-eight-hour period, faithful BlackBerry users had their own *War of the Worlds* experience. A software update glitch left millions of users without remote access to their e-mail. As R.E.M. would say, "It's the end of the world as we know it," but these users felt anything but fine. During this trying time, one man grew paranoid and distraught, thinking the malfunction millions were experiencing was, in fact, his staff of more than six hundred people quitting en masse in an act of protest against his necessary business trip to some tropical locale. The turmoil, the drama, the feeling of powerlessness. And all from something that sounds as natural as a fruit picked on a harmless, unhurried nature walk.

The man's temporary freak out, suffered by many of us in varying degrees even at the sight of one lonely service bar in a remote location on our cell phones, is a driving force behind the question, "Am I Missing Something?" Now, more than ever, we are rewarded for always trying to be more, yet far less so for determining when who we are and what we do is enough. How do we tell the moments when we have exerted enough time, energy, and spirit—when it's time to stop keeping up with *the* Joneses and *our* Joneses. The Bhaghavad Gita teaches that "the mind is indeed restless . . . but by constant practice and by freedom from passions [it] can in truth be trained." And yet it also teaches that a person's "former yearning and struggle irresistibly carries him onwards. And thus the Yogi ever-striving . . . attains perfection through many lives and reaches the End Supreme." So if passions induce striving, and striving brings us from life to life, and if we must go through enough lives to reach the End Supreme, is it ever okay just to . . . stop?

Some portion of finding your answer to this question is discovering what it is you're afraid you'll miss if you do stop, or at least slow down long enough to eat an actual blackberry, as opposed to living at the mercy of one. And isn't it odd that, with TiVo, DVR, and all things digital to capture every moment, not to mention channels devoted to "breaking news," which if you watch long enough are actually delivering the same stories over and over, we feel all the more like children absolutely adamant about not falling asleep lest we miss something really important? What might we be like if we freed ourselves from the notion that there is an ever-present "it" we are going to miss if we're not vigilant enough?

"Am I Missing Something?" is a trick question, in a sense, because it actually is a challenge to *stop* looking and to experience what is; to draw a distinction between the constructive passion that life demands and a destructive desire that demands more than we're able to give. The question hints at the essential difference between perpetually hunting for "the rest" and finding rest. "Am I Missing Something?" is the question that drives us to stop driving ourselves so hard, that asks us to create a counterpoint to the striving we can and must do as citizens of the world with the more difficult understanding that no world is complete without some form of respite. This is the equivalent of the "make-under" for life: what can you *not* do and enjoy the product?

Much of what drives this question comes from a sense that someone else is doing, being, or acquiring more than we are. We even compete for enlightenment and inner peace, power-yoga-ing our way to be more evolved and centered than the average Joe. And while adding "power" to yoga may be a relatively new phenomenon, the life-comparison-shopping experience is hardly original. As Goethe observed in *The Sorrows of Young Werther*:

> It is true that we are so made that we compare everything with ourselves and ourselves with everything. Therefore, our fortune or misfortune depends on the objects and persons to which we compare ourselves. . . . We so frequently feel that we are lacking many qualities which another person apparently possesses; and we then furnish such a person with everything we ourselves possess and with a certain idealistic complacency in addition. And in this fashion a Happy Being is finished to perfection—the creature of our imagination.

To take a page from Goethe's book, what is it that you, right now in this moment, believe exists "out there" in the life of another that drives you in a direction you might not otherwise take if you stopped to assess what is enough for you? Do you know for certain that the "Happy Being" you have conjured and fixed your sights on exists, or, at the very least, exists at the heart of who you are and what you care about most? Or are you off to see the Wizard, so far gone from knowing what feels like home to you that you wouldn't even know where you'd be going if you could get there just by clicking your heels? Have you, in your striving, in your constant state of motion, forgotten that the same things do not make everyone happy, but rather, as Spanish filmmaker Alejandro González Iñárritu observed just before the 2006 Cannes Film Festival premiere of *Babel*, "What makes us miserable is very, very similar."

Perhaps this is why the Declaration of Independence makes the pursuit of happiness, rather than happiness itself, an inalienable right. Simply having the ability to pursue, to hope, wish, expect, and look forward are essential human lifelines. But there are times when that same hoping can, as Proverbs teaches, sicken the heart without the occasional feeling that "desire realized is a tree of life." The pursuit of our desires is a lifeline, but so is gratitude for what we already have.

I was never a great science or math student, and only reluctantly took courses in those subjects to fulfill requirements in college. One of those classes was on the history of scientific revolutions, and much to my surprise I ended up loving it because it explored the evolution of ideas and the stories of dreamers, which involved a human equation I could understand without the help of six tutors.

One of the textbook assignments for the course

involved some of the most memorable reading I've ever done. The section recounted Christopher Columbus's aspiration to set sail across the Atlantic and circumnavigate the entire globe. Amerigo Vespucci and Magellan held the same aspirations, following in his ambitious wake. But, as I read, I discovered that Magellan died in the Phillipines and never made it home to complete his mission and bring it full circle. The first person to make the entire trip, landing at the same place he had begun after having circled the world on the sea, was a Malay slave, Enrique of Melaka, on Magellan's ship. While I had certainly heard of Columbus, Vespucci, and Magellan, Enrique of Melaka was new to me. Years later I would recall my unusually passionate encounter with Volume 2 of J. D. Bernal's *The Scientific and Industrial Revolutions* upon reading what has become now one of my most treasured Jewish teachings: that every person is the "amen," the punctuation mark, to the blessing of someone else's life. No matter how hard we push, or how far we get, we never finish our work. As much as we're here to make history, we're also here to leave a future upon which another generation of dreamers can build. Enrique of Melaka is hardly as well known as Columbus, but Columbus's dream only became fully realized when Enrique completed the circle Columbus began. He was the "amen" to a blessing and, in turn, set another blessing in motion for future explorers to punctuate with their own vision, courage, and daring.

Leaving room for the "amen" and finding your answer to "Am I Missing Something?" has to do with developing your own sense of what is enough amid your striving, so that you don't waste your time binging on things you don't want or need. Knowing this means understanding the division of destiny—knowing your place and focusing your efforts, rather than trying to be every place or every person. An ancient Talmudic saying, said to be a favorite among the sages, puts it best:

> I am God's creature and my fellow is God's creature. My work is in the town and his work is in the country. I rise early for my work and he rises early for his work. Just as he does not presume to do my work, so I do not presume to do his work.

Where is your portion—in the town or in the country? Is it in the silence of night when feet don't tread the sidewalks or the pavement but when your mind is most alive, or in the brightness of day when you are awake with possibilities long before most people have begged their alarm clocks for five more precious minutes of sleep? If you find your "work"—which does not necessarily mean finding your profession, but your place—you will also know when to take a step back from that work. You'll know when is enough.

Press Pause

Sean "Puff Daddy/P. Diddy/Diddy" Combs's latest musical effort, *Press Play*, is full of excellent gym music—perfect for running on the treadmill, keeping you moving when you're feeling like pressing "stop." But what is the soundtrack for answering whether you're missing something? What is the music that goes with learning how to value pressing "pause." That particular playlist may be silence—a sound all too easy to forget.

Italian conductor Riccardo Muti, otherwise known as "Maestro," was the musical director at the famed La Scala theater in Milan for nearly two decades before resigning in 2005 on the heels of a vote of no confidence by the workforce. In a fascinating interview with Muti in the *Financial Times* in March 2007, journalist Andrew Clark spoke with Muti about the highlights of his ambitious career. Muti talked at length about one memory in particular, the time he recorded Giuseppe Verdi's Requiem—a musical setting of the Roman Catholic funeral Mass—in the late 1970s. Perhaps it was no coincidence that he reflected upon that moment just as he was about to return to conduct the same setting in London the next day, more than three decades later.

Muti explained that he learned his interpretation of the Requiem from one of his mentors, conductor Vittorio Gui. At the time Gui was eighty-five and Muti was thirty. The Maestro commented specifically on the Requiem's concluding section, called "Libera me—Free me." Written into the score are the words *Lunga pausa*, or "long pause." This direction for the conductor comes just after the soprano has been pleading, according to Muti's loose translation, "Please, God, I'm defenseless, help me." Muti continued, "This is the drama of a modern man. The *lunga pausa* is part of the music, it's a vacuum of intensity—but most conductors are impatient, they like to move their arms. They ignore the pause and go on."

Where is the *lunga pausa* in your life? Where is the pause in the soundtrack of your striving that would be far easier to skip than to experience as part of the music you need to feel the movements of your existence are complete—if only for a moment? As the fourth-century Chinese philosopher Yang Chu warned in his *Garden of Pleasure*, "There are four things which do not allow people to rest: Long life. Reputation. Status. Wealth. Those who have these four things fear dead men and living men, power and punishment. They are always fugitives. Whether they are killed or whether they live, they spend their lives being controlled by external forces." Letting yourself be asked if you're missing something is letting yourself find the freedom to say you can rest, even when you know that an "infinity of things" is perpetually stretched before you. Where can you write the *lunga pausa* into your score so your life isn't all arm waving and BlackBerry scrolling, so that you aren't missing the beauty in the silence that makes the music all the more worth hearing?

There is so much to be said for what Russian poet Yunna Morits calls beginning to live "a little bit later"— for always living for a next day, another chance, another shot. Yet there is also something ominous to it, a delay that can hold all your days hostage if you never set aside at least one day to feel complete, to rest. In this sense, the poem cautions us against asking if we're missing something, as asking that way can work against us. Morits writes of crossing the river and moving through the forest, through everywhere, "not seeing what's in our sights, passing on. . . ." All this searching without living now.

Norah Jones, whose first album sold twenty million copies and garnered the young artist eight Grammys, and whose second effort sold ten million, offered her own wisdom on the *lunga pausa* she seems to have found for herself in an industry that is nothing if not about perpetually focusing on what will come next, what will be "a little bit later." Just after the release of her third effort, Jones said calmly in a *60 Minutes* interview, "I feel like I've had my cake, and I've eaten it, and I don't need another piece." I don't think she meant she wasn't hungry anymore, just that she had learned how to experience feeling satisfied.

It's Enough Already

At the end of the Jewish grace after having eaten a meal there is a phrase: "You ate and you were satisfied." The joining of these acts reminds us how often we eat, how stuffed we may get, but how we can still not feel satiated. If you never know the feeling of satiety, you cannot know whether your appetites are leading you toward the things you really want and need, or whether you're just eating for eating's sake.

I recall a chilling episode of *Grey's Anatomy* featuring a marathon runner who ignores his fatigue repeatedly throughout a race and swiftly finds himself on an operating-room table fighting for his life instead of celebrating his achievement. So focused on going the distance, the runner came close to losing not just a leg but his whole existence, all because he didn't know when stopping was what he was missing most. Cristina, the fiercely dedicated surgeon who would sooner drop dead before giving up an opportunity to scrub in on a complicated procedure, sees something frightening in the runner's story—and it isn't the blood, which she can more than handle. She sees the stakes of her own life in terms of an entirely different race she didn't realize she was running, but suddenly understands she wants and needs to finish. She is locked in a struggle of pride in her relationship with her boyfriend, Dr. Burke, such that they have created a contest to see who will speak to the other first and end their communications strike. After the surgery, Cristina decides to end her part of the silence. Out of her scrubs and sitting at the kitchen table, she looks at Burke and speaks for the first time in weeks, saying, "I'm in this. I'm in this for the long haul. And I'm in this to finish the race. So if that means I don't win this one, then fine, I don't win." In that moment, she understood—perhaps for the first time—that if you don't stop long enough to make sure you know why you're running or where you're sprinting to in the first place, life gets joyless, pleasureless, lonely, and moves way too fast.

It is this way for us all. If you don't stop long enough to evaluate where you want to be, you could end up at a finish line you didn't intend to reach. So the pause doesn't have to be a full stop, but there does have to be some kind of temporary suspension, some moment when you can say, as my grandma does, "It's enough already!" And mean it.

Asking "Am I Missing Something?" is learning how to answer with your own form of simulated perfection, your own placement of a finish line even when you know there are many miles yet to go. Think of yourself as Schubert's Eighth—or Unfinished—Symphony. The work is often called unfinished because some researchers believe that the two-movement work was meant to be part of four. And yet, the two movements stand on their own, none-theless. Because you are full of unlimited potential you will always have more music in you, and yet what you have already composed can stand on its own if you're willing to let it.

If you don't, instead of enjoying your symphony, you'll be trapped in what British band the Verve called the "Bitter Sweet Symphony." The video for the song says it best, with lead singer Richard Ashcroft walking down one unrecognizable street after another, totally numb to the fact that he's ploughing into people, walking through them as if they aren't there, completely unfazed by a woman who literally gets in his face and yells at him in a failed attempt to halt his zombie's tour of the world. Yet you get the sense that, even if he could hear the woman's cries, he couldn't stop even if he wanted to. It's clear he doesn't know how.

For all of his pioneering work as a social activist and his unceasing pursuit of human justice, Rabbi Abraham Joshua Heschel also spoke these words that have been passed through a powerful oral tradition even amid the pages and volumes of his staggering scholarly work. "Just to be is a blessing," he said, "just to live is holy." Heschel's statement is an essential part of an answer to the question of whether you or I or anyone is missing something, in that it challenges us to do something even harder than be more, but to learn how to just be.

One of Heschel's most famous works is *The Sabbath*, a commentary on the day of rest and its place in the rhythm of human life. Jewish tradition explains, rather counterintuitively, that creation was incomplete until rest was introduced into the mix. This means that one day out of every week, we find a way to see the world, our world, as whole, rather than as an array of scattered puzzle pieces that need our attention to be connected. We practice saying. "It's enough already." We live as if we need nothing else but exactly what is already there for that daylong period, what Heschel calls "an island in time." That day we hear the *lunga pausa* in the score. We remember that we don't have to buy a bottle of water to drink, but that refueling is as close and as easy as turning on the tap. That everything doesn't have to be hard-won to be rewarding.

It seems that some form of Sabbath exists in many religions, although you certainly needn't be religious to find your Sabbath. The themes of the existing models, though, can be helpful in finding your answer to "Am I Missing Something?" The Christian Sabbath is linked to the resurrection of Jesus, and carries its own question: What have you been neglecting in all of your striving that you need to bring back to life by slowing down and pulling back? The Muslim Sabbath corresponds to the creation of man on the sixth day, and raises another set of life-giving questions: For whom do you toil? Are you so busy that you've forgotten why you're here? And the Jewish Sabbath which, as I alluded to, is the finale to creation that curiously offers humanity its first opportunity to "do" something by ostensibly doing nothing, raising the challenge: Can you still be you if you let yourself know that the world will continue turning on its axis without your help for one day?

It's hard to resist the temptation to turn "Am I Missing Something?" into another call to raise the bar, squeeze more into the finite twenty-four-hour allotment we all get each day. But if you can find an answer that lets you learn how to create your day of enough, you might find that you don't feel quite as desperate to control time on the other days. Because you'll know why you do what you do, and for whom. You'll know what it feels like to eat *and* be satisfied, to leave a little bit left on the plate without feeling like everything's going to waste. You won't spend your time creating your own versions of the sequels we know we could have done without—*The Godfather: Part III, Rocky VI, Look Who's Talking Too*. Instead, you'll have the joy of what Van Morrison calls "Days Like This"— "when it's not always raining . . . when no one's complaining . . . when everything falls into place like the flick of a switch." It may take some practice and some imagination to make those days a reality, but they are yours if you want them.

It's true, as Heschel says in *The Sabbath*, that time is our greatest challenge, that it "is beyond our reach, beyond our power." Yet while we do not control time and we can never own it, we can own the moments in our lives. Owning those moments with joy and fulfillment begins with asking if you're missing something, and finding your own way, every once in a while, to say, "Not a thing."

YOUR HIGHLIGHTER

You will always find clues to locating your own answer if you use your highlighter—the internal power you have to know when an idea, an experience, a moment, another person's example—is resonating deeply with you, and, in the case of this question in particular, really giving you pause. Those are indicators of something inside you, something you're trying to tell yourself. These questions, based on the larger question we've just explored, are here to help you flick off the cap of that highlighter and find the answers that will work best in your life now.

- Where have you skipped the *lunga pausa* in the musical score of your life?

- What are you avoiding that might make skipping the *lunga pausa* more attractive?

- Have you evaluated what your finish line is lately? Is the life you're leading in line with where you want to go or is it sending you in another direction?

- What would a Sabbath of your own creation look like for you? What would you have to do to step back from your normal routine, to press Pause, to make a space in your life that says, "It's enough already?"

In the Beginning

*God is not finished. His highest divine attribute
is his creativeness and that which is creative exists
always in the beginning stage. God is eternally in
Genesis. And so are we.*

—Isaac Bashevis Singer, *Love in Exile*

I meant it when I said you could read this book out of order. For instance, if you're reading this part now, first, before you've looked at anything else, you'll find yourself at the beginning of taking hold of life's questions and trusting your answers. If you're a traditionalist and you started on page one, I also want to welcome you to a beginning. Because that is what life's best questions inspire: new paths, hidden gateways, open doors. They help you know what you want, what you need, and, most important, why you're needed. They tell you what your life is the answer to.

And that is why I hope you'll also come back to this page whenever you return to a question in this book, or when you add one of your own to it. In that first instant when you begin to see the question as a roadblock, a setback, the end of certainty and solidity, I hope you'll use this page to remind yourself that you are in genesis and that genesis is in you. I hope you'll remember that while the wisdom and contributions of others are an undeniable part of all of your answers, others are waiting for your wisdom to be a vital part of theirs. It could be one person, maybe many. But someone *is* waiting. I hope you'll recall that you, that we all, have a great deal to learn, but that there is not one person who does not have something to teach. And you are one of those people.

Find your life in the questions, not your self in someone else's answers. Believe that you can be the best living expert on *you*. You were born to do it.

Acknowledgments

Special thanks to David Kuhn for believing in this book, and to Abigail, whose rite of passage opened the door to a treasured one of my own. To John Duff and Meg Leder of Perigee for their passion, support, patience, skill, and ongoing enthusiasm for this project. To Rabbi Irving "Yitz" Greenberg and Rabbi Burton L. Visotzky. To my Papa, Grandpa Herb, Grandma Edith, and Leonard, all of blessed memory. To Ginger. To Robert, Penny, Max, Jake, and Zach. To Elli, Lauren, Chris, Roddy, Davide, Sybil, Martin, Felicia, Gabrielle, Tara, Rachel, Aaron, Elisa, Dasee, Leon, Nina, and Ruth. To Mom, Dad, and Phoebe, Stephanie, Eve, and Henry. With all my love and endless gratitude.

Sources of Wisdom

The Written Word

Aristotle. *The Nicomachean Ethics.* London: Penguin Classics, 2003.

Barks, Coleman. *The Soul of Rumi: A New Collection of Ecstatic Poems.* San Francisco, CA: HarperCollins, 2002.

Bernal, J. D. *Science in History—Volume 2: The Scientific and Industrial Revolutions.* Cambridge, MA: The M.I.T. Press, 1985.

Brant, Rosemary, ed. *Yang Chu's Garden of Pleasure.* Hod HaSharon, Israel: Astrolog Publishing House Ltd., 2005.

Bruner, Jerome. *Acts of Meaning.* Cambridge, MA: Harvard University Press, 1990.

Buber, Martin. *Tales of the Hasidim.* New York: Schocken Books, 1991.

Byrne, John A., with Lindsey Gerdes. "The Man Who Invented Management: Why Peter Drucker's Ideas Still Matter." *Business Week*, November 28, 2005.

Campbell, Joseph. *The Hero with a Thousand Faces.* Princeton, NJ: Princeton University Press, 1973.

Canan, Janine, ed. *Messages from Amma: In the Language of the Heart.* Berkeley, CA: Celestial Arts, 2004.

Carey, Benedict. "Do You Believe in Magic?" *New York Times*, January 23, 2007.

Clark, Andrew. "Passionate Believer in Pausing for Thought." *Financial Times*, March 6, 2007.

Coleman, Alexander, ed. *Jorge Luis Borges—Selected Poems*. New York: Viking, 1999.

Cooper, John M., ed. *Seneca: Moral and Political Essays*. Cambridge, UK: Cambridge University Press, 1995.

Dawood, N. J., trans. *The Koran*. London: Penguin Classics, 1999.

De Beauvoir, Simone. *The Ethics of Ambiguity*. New York: Citadel Press, 1976.

Didion, Joan. *The Year of Magical Thinking*. New York: Alfred A. Knopf, 2005.

Dreifus, Claudia. "Small Wonders: Understanding the Way of the Warrior Sperm." *New York Times*, January 23, 2007.

Eckhart, Meister. *Sermons and Treatises*. New York: Element Books, 1987.

Emerson, Ralph Waldo. *Essays: First and Second Series*. New York: Vintage Books, 1990.

Fitzgerald, Robert, trans. *The Odyssey*. New York: Vintage Classics, 1990.

Frankl, Viktor. *Man's Search for Meaning*. New York: Simon & Schuster, Inc., 1984.

Fromm, Erich. *The Art of Loving.* New York: Harper & Row, 1989.

Gibran, Kahlil. *The Prophet.* New York: Alfred A. Knopf, 1923.

Goethe, Johann Wolfgang von. *The Sorrows of Young Werther.* New York: Random House, Inc., 1971.

Grant, Douglas, ed. *Pope: Selected Poetry.* New York: Penguin Books, 1985.

Green, Arthur. *Tormented Master: The Life and Spiritual Quest of Rabbi Nahman of Bratslav.* Woodstock, NY: Jewish Lights Publishing, 1992.

Gunn, Battiscombe G., trans. *The Instruction of Ptah-Hotep and the Instruction of Ke'Gemni.* New York: E. P. Dutton and Company, 1908.

Harbage, Alfred, ed. *William Shakespeare—The Complete Works.* New York: Penguin Books, 1969.

Harvey, Simon, ed. *Votaire: Treatise on Tolerance.* Cambridge, UK: Cambridge University Press, 2004.

Heschel, Abraham Joshua. *The Sabbath: Its Meaning for Modern Man.* New York: Farrar, Straus and Giroux, 1993.

Heschel, Abraham Joshua. *Who Is Man?* Stanford, CA: Stanford University Press, 1965.

JPS Hebrew-English Tanakh. Philadelphia: The Jewish Publication Society, 2003. (*Please note*: Hebrew Bible references and quotations from this edition combine my own renderings of the Hebrew text and the English translations therein.)

Johnson, Thomas H., ed. *The Complete Poems of Emily Dickinson*. Boston: Back Bay Books, 1976.

Joyce, James. *Dubliners*. London: Penguin Books, 1992.

Kafka, Franz. *The Complete Stories*. New York: Schocken Books, 1971.

King Jr., Martin Luther. *A Knock at Midnight*. New York: Warner Books, 2001.

Krauss, Nicole. *The History of Love*. New York: W. W. Norton, 2006.

Lama, Dalai. *The Dalai Lama's Book of Wisdom*. New York: Thorsons, 2000.

L'Engle, Madeleine. *A Swiftly Tilting Planet*. New York: Farrar, Straus, Giroux, Inc., 1981

Lemonick, Michael D., and J. Madeleine Nash. "Cosmic Conundrum." *Time Magazine*, November 22, 2004.

Locke, John. "A Letter Concerning Toleration (1689)." www.constitution.org.

MacFarlane, Alan, and Gerry Martin. *Glass: A World History*. Chicago: University of Chicago Press, 2002.

Maimonides, Moses. *Pirkei Avot—Shemoneh Perakim of the Rambam*. Brooklyn, NY: Moznaim, 1994.

Maitreya, Ananda, trans. *The Dhammapada*. Berkeley, CA: Parallax Press, 1995.

Malamud, Bernard. *The Complete Stories.* New York: Farrar, Straus and Giroux, 1998.

Mascaro, Juan, trans. *The Bhaghavad Gita.* London: Penguin Books, 1962.

Michaels, Axel. *Hindusim: Past and Present.* Princeton, NJ: Princeton University Press, 2004.

Milton, John. *The Complete Poems.* London: Penguin Classics, 1999.

Paine, Thomas. *Common Sense.* New York: Penguin Books, 2004.

Penington, Isaac. *The Works of Isaac Penington.* Glenside, PA: Quaker Heritage Press, 1996.

Pine-Coffin, R. S., trans. *St. Augustine: Confessions of a Sinner.* London: Penguin Books, 2004.

Reed, Bika, trans. *Rebel in the Soul: An Ancient Egyptian Dialogue Between Man and His Destiny.* Vermont: Inner Traditions International, 1997.

Robbins, Liz. "112 Points a Game At 90 M.P.H." *New York Times,* January 24, 2007.

Sandmel, Samuel, ed. *The New English Bible with the Apocrypha.* New York: Oxford University Press, 1972. (*Please note*: New Testament references and quotations are drawn from this English translation.)

Schopenhauer, Arthur. *On the Suffering of the World.* London: Penguin Group, 2004.

Sears, Priscilla. "Wangari Maathai: 'You Strike the Woman.'" *In Context*, Spring 1991.

Setzer, Claudia. *The Quotable Soul: Inspiring Quotations Crossing Time and Culture*. New York: John Wiley & Sons, Inc., 1994.

Simon, Maurice, trans. *Midrash Rabbah*. London: Soncino Press, 1983.

Simon, Maurice, trans. *Talmud Bavli*. London: Soncino Press, 1984.

Simon, Maurice, trans. *The Zohar*. London: Soncino Press, 1984.

Sloane Coffin, William. *A Passion for the Possible*. Louisville, KY: Westminster John Knox Press, 2007.

Smith, Patti. "Ain't it Strange." *New York Times*, March 12, 2007.

Smith, Zadie. *White Teeth*. New York: Random House, 2000.

Spinoza, Benedict de. *A Theologio-Political Treatise*. New York: Dover Publications, Inc., 1951.

Tagore, Rabindranath Sir. *Stray Birds*. London: Hesperides Press, 2006.

Thamel, Pete. "'Unhealthy' Obsession Has Led to Success." *New York Times*, March 22, 2007.

Tallmer, Jerry. "Billy Joel Grapples with the Past." *The Villager*, July 16–22, 2003.

Wallach, Amei. "New 'Truisms' in Words and Light." *New York Times*, September 28, 2005.

Weil, Simone. *Waiting for God*. New York: Harper Perennial, 2001.

Wittenberg, Jonathan. *The Three Pillars of Judaism*. Harrisburg, PA: Trinity Press International, 1997.

Wolfe, Tom. *The Electric Kool-Aid Acid Test*. New York: Bantam Books, 1980.

Wyatt, Edward. "A Sitcom That's All About Me, Sarah." *New York Times*, January 31, 2007.

Music

Alanis Morissette, "That I Would be Good," 1998. *Supposed Former Infatuation Junkie*. Maverick, CD.

Alice Cooper, "I'm Eighteen," 1971. *Love It to Death*. Warner Brothers, CD.

Alice Cooper, "School's Out," 1972. *School's Out*. Warner Brothers, CD.

Barbra Streisand, "What Are You Doing the Rest of Your Life," 1974. *The Way We Were*. Sony, CD.

Billie Holiday, "God Bless the Child," 1995. *God Bless the Child*. MCA Special Products, CD.

Billy Joel, "Vienna," 1977. *The Stranger*. Sony, CD.

Broadway Cast, "I Hope I Get It," 1975. *A Chorus Line*. Sony, CD.

Broadway Cast, "A Quiet Thing," 1965. *Flora, the Red Menace*. RCA Victor Broadway, CD.

Charlie Tillman, "Gimme That Old Time Religion," 1891. Multiple variations.

Dionne Warwick, "Alfie," 1989. *The Dionne Warwick Collection: Her All-Time Greatest Hits.* Rhino/Wea, CD.

Don Henley, "The Heart of the Matter," 1989. *The End of the Innocence.* UMG Recordings Inc., CD.

Foo Fighters, "Best of You," 2005. *In Your Honor.* Roswell, CD.

Frank Sinatra, "It Was a Very Good Year," 1965. *September of My Years.* Warner, CD.

The Fray, "Over My Head (Cable Car)," 2005. *How to Save a Life.* Sony BMG Music Entertainment, CD.

Gnarls Barkley, "Crazy," 2006. *St. Elsewhere.* Downtown, CD.

Goo Goo Dolls, "Iris," 1998. *Dizzy Up the Girl.* Warner, CD.

Gregg Allman, "I'm No Angel," 1986. *I'm No Angel.* Sony, CD.

Guns N' Roses, "Welcome to the Jungle," 1989. *Appetite for Destruction.* Geffen Records, CD.

Harry Connick Jr. (with Kim Burrell), "All These People," 2007. *Oh, My Nola.* Sony BMG Music Entertainment, CD.

James Ingram (with Patti Austin), "How Do You Keep the Music Playing," 1991. *James Ingram—The Greatest Hits.* Warner, CD.

Johnny Cash, "I Walk the Line," 1969. *At San Quentin.* Sony, CD.

Judy Collins, "Both Sides Now," 1967. *Wildflowers.* Elektra, CD.